Anna Bicknell

Life in the Tuileries under the second empire

Anna Bicknell

Life in the Tuileries under the second empire

ISBN/EAN: 9783337274146

Printed in Europe, USA, Canada, Australia, Japan

Cover: Foto ©ninafisch / pixelio.de

More available books at **www.hansebooks.com**

LIFE IN THE TUILERIES
UNDER THE SECOND EMPIRE

EUGÉNIE

FROM A LITHOGRAPH OF WINTERHALTER'S PAINTING, "EUGÉNIE AND HER COURT."

LIFE IN THE TUILERIES UNDER THE SECOND EMPIRE

BY
ANNA L. BICKNELL
AN INMATE OF THE PALACE

NEW YORK
THE CENTURY CO.
1895

CONTENTS

CHAPTER I

PAGE

The palace of the Tuileries under previous sovereigns — Proclamation of the Second Empire — The Comte de Tascher de la Pagerie — Napoleon I. and Josephine — Ball given by Prince Schwarzenberg on the marriage of Napoleon I. with Marie-Louise — Tragic fate of the Princess von der Leyen — Her daughter married to the Comte de Tascher de la Pagerie — Exile after the fall of the First Empire — Prince Eugène de Beauharnais — Queen Hortense — Napoleon III. in his youth — His friendship for the Comte de Tascher de la Pagerie — When President of the French Republic he summons the Comte and his son to the Élysée — Their opposition to his marriage with Eugénie de Montijo overruled — Court of the Empress Eugénie 1

CHAPTER II

My position at the Tuileries — The family de Tascher de la Pagerie — First opportunities of seeing the Empress — Her wonderful beauty — The color of her hair — An evening with the Empress in her private circle — Unseasonable interruption — Etiquette and its annoyances — Court obligations — Gilded chains 13

CHAPTER III

Regulations of the palace — The detectives — Inconveniences of the palace — The painting-room of Mademoiselle Hortense de Tascher — Pasini, the artist — Apartments of the Empress — View on the garden of the Tuileries — What it was then — Description of the various rooms — Audiences granted by the Empress — High mass on Sundays — The Emperor's demeanor — The sermon — Etiquette — The wardrobe regions above the apartments of the Empress — "Pepa," the Empress's Spanish maid — The jailer's daughters — Anecdote of the Emperor — The privy-purse of the Empress 29

CHAPTER IV

Daily life of the Court — Duties of the ladies in waiting — Charities of the Emperor and Empress — The Prince Imperial — Drives of the Empress — A rheumatic chamberlain — The evenings at the court — Dinner — The "service d'honneur" — Etiquette — Habitual simplicity of the Empress in her morning-dress — Her usual evening toilet — The mechanical piano — Sudden wish of the Empress to dance the "Lancers" — Mademoiselle de Tascher summoned to teach the figures — Difficulties caused by petty court jealousies — Late hours of the Empress — Anecdote of the Emperor — His amiable disposition in private life — Impulsive nature of the Empress. 42

CHAPTER V

The Emperor's drives — His opinion of mankind in general — The special police attached to the Emperor's person — Alessandri, the detective — The Orsini attempt on the Emperor's life — Impression at the Tuileries — The return of the Emperor and Empress — Letter from the Marquis of Waterford — My life at the Tuileries — Games of chess with the Archbishop of Bourges — Costume balls — Banquet on the marriage of Prince Napoleon with the Princess Clotilde of Savoy — The ball — A waltz of the Emperor with the Princess rendered impossible — Costume of the Empress .. 52

CHAPTER VI

The Palais-Royal — The imperial family — Unpleasant relations — Prince Jerome — Prince Napoleon — Princess Mathilde — Pierre Bonaparte — His sister Letitia — Prince

Napoleon's speech in the Senate — Scene with the Emperor — Ball at the Hôtel d'Albe — The Empress and the page — Special invitation sent to me by the Empress — Princess Mathilde and Princess Clotilde — Contrast — The dresses of both — Intended costume of the Empress — Objections — The Empress and the paste-board horse — The Duc de Morny — His character — His marriage — Madame de Morny — "The White Mouse" — Scene with the Duc de Dino — Comte Walewski — His character and appearance — Comtesse Walewska.................................... 62

CHAPTER VII

Princess Clotilde — Her religious fervor — Her daily life — Her court — Evenings at the Palais-Royal — Ennui of the Empress Eugénie — The camp at Châlons — Enmity of the aristocratic Faubourg St. Germain — Persistent criticisms; irritation of the Empress — The Comte de Chambord and the Comtesse de Tascher — The great official balls at the Tuileries — The "Centgardes" — The soldier with sugar-plums in his boot — The Empress and the sentinel — A wager — Etiquette of the balls — The balcony of the "Salle des Maréchaux" — Clever answer of Mademoiselle de Montijo — Costume balls — The police — The fancy quadrilles — Taglioni 78

CHAPTER VIII

The police force during the Empire — Story of M. de Saint-Julien — A robbery — A fascinating detective — A mysterious sign — Dinner parties at the palace — The imperial table during Lent and on Fridays — Lent concerts — Auber — Mario — Patti — Alboni — The national tune composed by Queen Hortense — The Emperor's dislike of music — The mechanical piano — The "Stabat Mater" performed in the chapel — The supposed excessive devotion of the Empress. 89

CHAPTER IX

"The Empress's Mondays" — Orders worn by ladies — The court train — The "Salut du Trône," or grand court obeisance — The inclosed garden at the Tuileries — "Bagatelle"

— The court leaves Paris — Fontainebleau — "La Régie" — Inconvenience of living in a palace — Housewifely care of the Empress — A siege in the apartments — A prince left at the door — St. Cloud — Villeneuve l'Étang — Furniture embroidered by Josephine — A collation with the Prince Imperial — Anecdotes — A "Te Deum" wanted 98

CHAPTER X

The great review — Canrobert — MacMahon — The Zouaves — The flag with the ribbon and cross of the Legion of Honor — Violent rush of the crowd — I owe my life to Robert de Tascher — Court starvation on gala days 111

CHAPTER XI

Paris in the early days of the Second Empire — Diplomatic changes after the Italian war — A great name — A young ambassadress — Eccentricities of the Princess Metternich — Her imprudence and morbid curiosity — Anecdotes — A "real" Empress — Practical joke on a lady in waiting — Dispute with Madame de Persigny — Why the Princess Metternich could not yield to her — Count Sandor — His strange exploits — Practical joke on his old housekeeper — Imperial hospitality at Compiègne — Dresses required for the week's visit — Daily life of the visitors — Kindness of the Imperial hosts — Five o'clock tea in the private apartments of the Empress — Evenings — Questionable diversions provided by the Princess Metternich — Exaggerated reports — Personal description of the Princess Metternich — General Fleury 116

CHAPTER XII

"Golden Wedding" of the Comte and Comtesse de Tascher de la Pagerie — Curious story of a lost ring — Marriage of my elder pupil — Prince Maximilian von Thurn und Taxis — Death of the Comte de Tascher — Kindness and affectionate attentions of the Emperor and Empress during his last illness — Sorrow of the Emperor — The Count laid out in state — Effect on the Empress — Her nervous condition —

Her private sorrows — She begins to interfere in political matters — Our home life after the death of the Comte de Tascher — Home evenings — Weekly receptions — Ambassadors Extraordinary from Oriental lands — The Persian Ambassador — The Embassy from Siam — Reception at Fontainebleau — The hair-dresser Leroy.................. 131

CHAPTER XIII

The little Prince Imperial — The Emperor's excessive indulgence — Vain efforts of the Empress "to bring up that child properly" — The Empress and the pony — The Emperor and the orange — Amiable disposition of the Prince — His efforts to "earn money for the poor" — General Frossard's military discipline — Anecdotes — The "honor of the uniform" — The Prince takes the measles — Seriously ill — Nursed by the Empress with the greatest maternal devotion 144

CHAPTER XIV

The military element in Parisian society — Pélissier and Canrobert — Anecdotes of the former — How he treated a coward — A defective omelet and its consequences — His uncivilized manners — His marriage — The Duchesse de Malakoff — Canrobert — His marriage — Madame Canrobert — Pretensions of the marshal checked by the Emperor — An apparently ill-assorted but happy pair — Honorable character of Canrobert — MacMahon — Castellane — Magnan — Bosquet — Characteristic anecdote of the Emperor — Vaillant — Randon — Three inappropriate Christian names — Bazaine 151

CHAPTER XV

Monsieur Thouvenel — A French ambassador at Constantinople — A night spent in Oriental luxury — Its questionable delights — A parrot's reprimand to an ambassador — Monsieur Thouvenel, Minister of Foreign Affairs — Policy of Monsieur Thouvenel — Opposition of the Emperor and Empress — The Emperor's speech on opening the Legislative Assembly — Feeling of the nation — Thouvenel obliged to resign — The child and the Emperor — Generosity of the latter — Petition of a Legitimist lady — Plain speaking — Chivalrous conduct of the Emperor — His noble nature.... 160

CHAPTER XVI

Clouds in the sky of the Empire — The Mexican war unpopular — "L'Empire, c'est la paix!" — Financial difficulties — Extravagant tendencies of the Emperor — The yacht built for the Empress — The Hôtel d'Albe built and destroyed — Expenses of Compiègne and Fontainebleau — Costly artistic mistakes — The Emperor's lavish generosity — Too many improvements in Paris — Spanish preferences of the Empress — She goes to bull-fights — The Empress goes to Spain — Death of the Duc de Morny 168

CHAPTER XVII

Evenings in the apartments of the Duchesse de Tascher — Madame Ristori, the tragic actress — How a stage queen ate asparagus — Her conversation — Sixteen thousand pounds of luggage — Danger in a glass of lemonade — Recitations — The real dress of Queen Mary on the scaffold — Madame Ristori's impersonation of Mary Stuart — The evil eye — The value of stage bouquets as a mark of public enthusiasm — Leopold von Mayer — How he played the piano with his fists — He plays before the Sultan — Death of the Archbishop of Bourges — The Papal Nuncio — Prince Chigi — Djemil Pasha, the Turkish Ambassador — Marriage of Hortense de Tascher to the Comte de l'Espine 180

CHAPTER XVIII

I leave the Tuileries — Opinion in the provinces — The Empress severely judged — Exaggerated reports — Intimacy with Metternich and Nigra — Why the Emperor disapproved — Opinion expressed by the Duc de Tascher on the Empress, before her marriage — Outbreak of the cholera — Her admirable conduct — How an Empress "stands fire" —

Nature and education of the Empress Eugénie — The Empress Augusta of Germany — The Empress Eugénie visits charitable institutions — Mlle. Bouvet — The Empress visits the poor — Goes to Belleville and other dangerous places — Excellent intentions not always wisely carried out — Successful interference in the Penitentiary for Juvenile Offenders 188

CHAPTER XIX

Hints in the papers on the Emperor's health — The cost of a crown — Visits to provincial towns — Uncomfortable luxury — The true color of the Empress's hair — The great exhibition — Death of the Emperor Maximilian — Death of the Duc de Tascher and of the Duchesse de Bassano — The Empress goes to the opening of the Suez Canal — Effect on the Mohammedan population — The Emperor and Prince Imperial at Compiègne — My visit to the Tuileries in 1870 — Physical condition of the Emperor — The plebiscite — Testimony of Lord Malmesbury — I leave Paris with sad forebodings — The palace of the Tuileries when I next saw it.. 200

CHAPTER XX

Apathy of the Emperor — The party of the Empress — A consultation of medical and surgical authorities on the Emperor's health — An operation declared necessary — The Hohenzollern incident — The Emperor unwilling for war — The scene at St. Cloud related to Lord Malmesbury by the Duc de Gramont — The Emperor yields — His sad forebodings — The Empress appointed Regent — The Prince Imperial goes with his father to join the army — The "baptism of fire" — First reverses — The Empress returns to Paris — The Emperor's health gives way — He is urged to return to Paris — Opposition of the Empress — The Emperor sends the Prince Imperial to Belgium — The Emperor goes to Sedan against his will — The Prince Imperial receives orders to go over to England, where he meets his mother at Hastings................................ 212

CONTENTS

CHAPTER XXI

MacMahon leads the army to Sedan — Despair of the Emperor — He vainly seeks death — He gives up his sword to the King of Prussia — Telegram to the Empress — Confusion and treachery around her — The Princess Clotilde comes to share her danger — The ambassadors of Austria and Italy offer their protection — She goes with them, followed only by Madame Lebreton — The Empress and Madame Lebreton left to their fate in a hackney-carriage. 224

CHAPTER XXII

The Empress applies to Dr. Evans in her distress — Leaves Paris in his carriage — A perilous journey — The arrival at Trouville — Sir John Burgoyne and his sailing-yacht, the *Gazelle* — Consents to take the Empress over to England — A perilous undertaking — Tremendous storm — Safe arrival at Ryde — The Empress meets her son at Hastings — Hires a furnished country house at Chiselhurst — The Emperor a prisoner at Wilhelmshöhe — His patience and kindness 234

CHAPTER XXIII

The Emperor in England — Visit of Lord Malmesbury — His impression of the interview — The Commune in Paris — What the leaders really were — Burning of the Tuileries — How effected 243

CONCLUSION

The Empress and her son settle at Camden Place, Chiselhurst — The Emperor joins them after the peace — First difficulties — Education of the Prince Imperial — Woolwich — Hopes of a restoration of the Empire — The Emperor's health — His unexpected death — The Prince receives a large number of Imperialists on his coming of age — Passes his examination satisfactorily at Woolwich — His life at Chiselhurst — Difficulties — Hopes — He determines to join the English army in South Africa — His departure — His reckless bravery — He is killed in a reconnoissance — Particulars of his death — Announcement of the news to the Empress — Her journey to Zululand — Her present life. .. 251

LIST OF ILLUSTRATIONS

Eugénie..............................Frontispiece	
	FACING PAGE
The Tuileries from the Place du Carrousel.........	8
General Comte de Tascher de la Pagerie; Princess Amélie von der Leyen, Comtesse de Tascher de la Pagerie; and Duc de Tascher.................	16
Empress Eugénie wearing a Spanish Mantilla........	32
Napoleon III. and the Empress Eugénie ..	40
Garden Front of the Tuileries.......................	48
Prince Jerome and Princess Mathilde................	56
Prince Napoleon and Princess Clotilde..............	64
Duc de Morny and Duchesse de Morny.	72
Comte de Walewski and Prince Napoleon..	80
Napoleon III., Empress Eugénie, and Prince Imperial.	96
Marshal Canrobert and Marshal MacMahon.........	112
Empress Eugénie, 1863.............................	128
The Prince Imperial...............................	144
Duc de Malakoff and Duchesse de Malakoff.........	152

	FACING PAGE
Marshal Castellane and Marshal Randon	160
Duchess of Alva and Children	176
The Rue de Rivoli during the Burning of the Tuileries	192
Gallery of Peace, Ruins of the Tuileries	208
Ruins of the Hall of the Marshals, Caryatides of the Throne on the Right	224
Ruins of the Vestibule of the Tuileries	240
The Pavilion of Flora after the Fire	248
The Prince Imperial, in Artillery Uniform	272

LIFE IN THE TUILERIES
UNDER THE SECOND EMPIRE

LIFE IN THE TUILERIES
UNDER THE SECOND EMPIRE

❦

CHAPTER I

The palace of the Tuileries under previous sovereigns—Proclamation of the Second Empire—The Comte de Tascher de la Pagerie—Napoleon I. and Josephine—Ball given by Prince Schwarzenberg on the marriage of Napoleon I. with Marie-Louise—Tragic fate of the Princess von der Leyen—Her daughter married to the Comte de Tascher de la Pagerie—Exile after the fall of the First Empire—Prince Eugène de Beauharnais—Queen Hortense—Napoleon III. in his youth—His friendship for the Comte de Tascher de la Pagerie—When President of the French Republic he summons the Comte and his son to the Elysée—Their opposition to his marriage with Eugénie de Montijo overruled—Court of the Empress Eugénie.

THE beautiful palace built by Catherine de Medicis, and afterward enlarged by the succeeding royal owners, was not, at first, a favorite residence of the French kings. With the exception of a short period during the minority of Louis XV., it was not permanently inhabited by the Court before the French Revolution, at which time Louis XVI. and Marie Antoinette were forcibly brought there from Versailles; being detained in a sort of captivity till the fatal insurrection of August 10, 1792, when the mob broke into the palace and massacred the Swiss guards, while the royal family took refuge in the Legislative Assembly, whence they were taken as prisoners to the Temple tower.

When Napoleon Bonaparte became First Consul, and while Emperor, he preferred the Tuileries to the immense palace of Versailles, which, in those days of slow conveyances, was at an inconvenient distance from Paris, and ordered the apartments to be prepared with great magnificence for the requirements of his Court.

Louis XVIII. followed his example after the restoration of the Bourbons; the Tuileries palace was splendidly furnished and ready for occupation, while Versailles, having been pillaged and much injured, could only be made habitable at great expense. Napoleon said sarcastically on this occasion: "If Louis is wise, he will use my bed-chamber, and sleep in my bed, for it is a good one." The King was wise, and unconsciously followed the ironical advice.

The court was now definitely established at the Tuileries, which was inhabited, after the fall of Charles the Tenth, by Louis Philippe and his family, during the whole of the latter's reign.

After the revolution of 1848, and the flight of Louis Philippe, the mob again broke into the palace of the Tuileries, where the royal apartments were pillaged. The throne, carried in triumph by the populace, was burned; total destruction was feared, but was happily prevented by the Provisional Government, who declared the Tuileries national property.

From this time the palace remained uninhabited till the *coup d'état* of Louis Napoleon, then President of the French Republic. In January, 1852, Napoleon removed from the Elysée to the Tuileries, which, a few months later, on December 2, 1852, he solemnly reëntered as Emperor, passing under the triumphal arch of the principal entrance, adorned with the inscriptions: "Vox Populi, vox Dei!" "Ave Cæsar, Imperator!"

And yet people will talk seriously of the "Will of the nation"! Could any one who witnessed the wild enthusiasm of the first days of the Second Empire doubt its sincerity? And yet what a fall after eighteen years of prosperity!

Nearly two months later, on January 22, 1853, the new Emperor convened all the great functionaries of the state in the throne-room of the Tuileries. There he announced his intended marriage,—a marriage in opposition to all the traditions of his predecessors—a circumstance which, with his characteristic adroitness, he contrived to present as having great advantages over ordinary princely unions. All were astonished. No one, however, had any time for opposition, if such had been intended; for only a week after the official announcement had been made to the representatives of the nation, the civil marriage took place at the Tuileries, preceding, according to custom, the religious ceremony, which was celebrated on the following day at Notre Dame. The young Empress, who had remained at the Elysée during the interval, then returned in state to the Tuileries, and appeared, in her white robe and veil, on the fated balcony of the "Salle des Maréchaux," where so many princesses had stood—the last royal bride who would ever be seen there.

The marriage of the ambitious heir of the great Napoleon with Eugénie de Montijo (who, though descended from the illustrious race of Guzman, was not of royal blood) astonished the world, and none more than his most faithful and devoted adherents, among whom were the whole family de Tascher de la Pagerie, his oldest friends and relatives.

The Comte de Tascher de la Pagerie, first cousin to the Empress Josephine, had been called to the court of Napoleon I. when scarcely more than a boy in years, and soon became a great favorite, not only of Josephine, but also of the great Emperor himself, whom he followed in his campaigns, but more especially under the command of his cousin Prince Eugène de Beauharnais, who was the son of Josephine de Tascher de la Pagerie, by her first marriage with the Comte de Beauharnais, guillotined during the French Revolution.

The affection of both Napoleon and Josephine for the spirited and chivalrous young officer survived their divorce; and at the time of Napoleon's marriage with Marie-Louise, the young Comte de Tascher de la Pagerie was betrothed, with the Emperor's approval, to the Princess Amélie von der Leyen, daughter of the mediatized[1] Prince von der Leyen. The marriage took place, but under particularly disastrous circumstances.

It may be remembered that the ball given by the Austrian ambassador, Prince Schwarzenberg, in honor of the imperial nuptials was the scene of a frightful catastrophe. The hangings of the ball-room having caught fire, the flames spread to the whole building, and many victims perished, amongst whom were the Princess Schwarzenberg herself, and the Princess von der Leyen, both in the attempt to save their daughters. The Princess Amélie was dancing with her future husband when the fire broke out; he at once placed her in safety, returning to seek her mother, who meanwhile had been taken away from the ball-room, but who, like the Princess Schwarzenberg, rushed back into the flames to find her daughter. A burning beam had fallen on her, and, when found, her condition was absolutely hopeless. She was extricated with the greatest difficulty; the heat around her had been so intense that the silver setting of her diamonds had melted into the burned flesh. Strange to say, a few flowers of a wreath she wore had escaped the flames, and the writer of these pages has often seen them, set in a frame, under the portrait of the unfortunate Princess, in the bed-

[1] The mediatized Princes of the Holy Roman Empire had yielded their petty states by the Rhine Treaties, but retained the social rank and privileges of independent sovereigns, with the title of "Serene Highness."

chamber of her daughter. She lived two or three days in fearful suffering, but insisted on the marriage ceremony taking place at once by her deathbed. And in the presence of the dying mother, who had sacrificed her life for her daughter's safety, Amélie von der Leyen was united to Louis de Tascher de la Pagerie.

The fall of the First Empire destroyed the brilliant prospects of the young pair. Louis XVIII. offered an important post at his court to the Comte de Tascher de la Pagerie; but imbued with the principle expressed in his family motto, "Honori fidelis," he rejected all advances, even from those who, as legitimate possessors, filled the throne of the emperor to whom he had sworn allegiance, and therefore chose to follow his cousin Prince Eugène de Beauharnais, who, having married a princess of Bavaria, had elected Munich as his residence in exile. The sister of Prince Eugène, Hortense (who was separated from her husband, Louis Bonaparte, king of Holland), had accepted the title of "Duchesse de Saint-Leu," and wandered from one place of residence to another with her two sons, the younger of whom was afterward known as Napoleon III.

Louis de Tascher remained on terms of the greatest affection and intimacy with Queen Hortense, and after the death of her brother, Prince Eugène, he became her most trusted friend and counselor.

His sons and daughters, who were often invited to stay at Arenenberg, on the lake of Constance (where she finally resided habitually), were the playfellows of her sons in their childhood, and the friends of Louis Napoleon when, by the death of his elder brother, he became the head of the Bonaparte family, and the representative of what they held to be their rights. The light-hearted girls and merry boys of the de Tascher family brought some life to the too quiet home of Queen Hortense, where the future emperor, always absorbed in thought, was then, as in after life, a gentle dreamer, scarcely roused to a smile by the vivacious ways and lively jests of his young cousins, who, as they afterward acknowledged, could not help, even then, feeling inwardly a sort of awe in his presence, as in that of a superior being.

When the end of Queen Hortense drew near, she summoned the Comte de Tascher to her bedside, to receive her last instructions and hear her last wishes. He it was who attended to all that was needful after her death; who obtained from the government of Louis Philippe the requisite permission to bring back the remains of the exiled queen to her native land; and who followed them to their last resting-place at Rueil, near Paris. There was, consequently, a strong tie of affection, confidence, and respect between Prince Louis Napoleon and his mother's relative and trusted friend. When his strangely varied fortunes brought him to that supreme position which he had always anticipated in what seemed idle dreams, he immediately called the Comte de Tascher de la Pagerie, and his surviving son, to his bachelor court at the Elysée; the ladies of the family remained, temporarily, at Munich.

The Comte de Tascher had always felt the importance of a suitable marriage for Prince Louis Napoleon, and had greatly exerted himself to negotiate several which he approved, and which had been nearly concluded. One, in the early youth of the Prince, with the Princess Mathilde, his cousin, sister of Prince (Jerome) Napoleon, had been settled by family arrangements, but was broken off, after the failure of the Strasburg conspiracy. Other negotiations, undertaken by the Comte de Tascher personally, in the hope of obtaining the hand of several German princesses, had fallen through, in consequence of the ill-will of their respective courts.

The Comte de Tascher still hoped, nevertheless, that the rising fortunes of the Prince, now President of the French Republic, would finally conquer all difficulties; but the mere idea that, as Emperor (a destiny which all foresaw), he would marry the beautiful Spanish girl with whom, as President, he flirted at Compiègne, never seriously dwelt in the mind of the devoted friend of early days. When, immediately after the proclamation of the Empire, the intentions of the new Emperor were communicated privately to the Comte de Tascher and his son, they were so painfully surprised that they warmly remonstrated as to the complications which would be added to his already difficult position, by the act of raising to the throne of France a private gentlewoman (how-

THE TUILERIES FROM THE PLACE DU CARROUSEL.

FROM A PHOTOGRAPH.

ever attractive she might be), without consulting the will of the nation. They reminded him that the case of Josephine, to which he referred, was not to be quoted as parallel; she was more than her husband's equal when she married him, and had risen with him. As the Emperor would listen to no expostulation, they finally declared that if he persisted in his intentions they would leave him and return to Germany.

At this, the Emperor, who was pacing the room, suddenly turned round, exclaiming with unusual vehemence:

"So, because you look upon me as a drowning man, you will leave me, and refuse to give me a helping hand?"

This was startling and painful; they were silenced. The Emperor then made a strong appeal to their feelings of old friendship and personal attachment, to induce them not only to welcome his bride, but to accept the two most important posts in her future court. The General Comte de Tascher de la Pagerie was appointed "Grand Master of the Empress's Household," and his son, then called "Count Charles," became First Chamberlain.

The Empress was fully aware of their conscientious opposition to her marriage, which, naturally, caused some constraint at first; but her own sincere nature soon appreciated the noble and chivalrous character of the old Count, and the honest devotedness of his son, when once they had given their allegiance. The ladies of the family then came to the Tuileries, where apartments were provided for them, and where the Emperor received them on their arrival with the most unaffected kindness, recalling heartily old times and bygone recollections.

The splendor of the First Empire now reappeared at the Tuileries. The Comte de Tascher would have preferred a mere military household for the Emperor, and the strictly necessary number of ladies for the Empress; but Napoleon III. was determined to revive the court of Napoleon I., with its somewhat obsolete magnificence.

There was a Great Chamberlain, the Duc de Bassano, who resided at the palace in the Pavillon Marsan (formerly inhabited by the Duc d'Orléans and Duc de Nemours, sons of Louis Philippe). The apartments of the Duc de Bassano were those which had belonged to the Duc de Nemours. The Empress had a "Grand Maître," the Comte de Tascher de la Pagerie, two chamberlains, an equerry, six ladies-in-waiting (afterward increased to twelve), a "Dame d'honneur," or First Lady, and a "Grande Maîtresse," the Princesse d'Essling. The "Dame d'honneur" was the Duchesse de Bassano; the others were often erroneously called "dames d'honneur" by the uninitiated, but were properly entitled "Dames du Palais," or "Ladies of the Palace."

The Duchesse de Bassano did not, like the others, take regular turns of "waiting" on the Empress, but appeared on ceremonious occasions, taking the first rank, shared with the Princesse d'Essling, who was entitled "Grande Maîtresse of the Empress's Household." On state visits to the opera, with foreign princes and princesses, the Duchesse de Bassano and the Princesse d'Essling took turns to stand behind the chair of the Empress during the whole evening, each for half an hour at a time. The Duchesse de Bassano told me that this was very trying, as there was, of course, no possibility of leaning on any support, and they must stand motionless. At the receptions of ambassadors, and other state occasions, all the ladies appeared around the Empress, but the Duchesse de Bassano was always at their head. The three principal ladies were the Princesse d'Essling, the Duchesse de Bassano, and Madame Bruat[1], widow of l'Amiral Bruat, who was state-governess to the Prince Imperial, or, as she was formally entitled, " Gouvernante des Enfants de France," a great source of exasperation to the Legitimists, who claimed the title of " Fils de France " exclusively for the Comte de Chambord. These three ladies, who held the rank of " grand officier," wore the portrait of the Empress set in diamonds, hanging from a knot of ribbon fastened on the left shoulder. The other "ladies-in-waiting" wore in the same manner the monogram of the Empress, IE (Eugénie Impératrice), in small diamonds, on an enamel ground. The Comte Charles de Tascher de la Pagerie was First Chamberlain. He had

[1] Appointed on the birth of the Prince Imperial.

already inherited the title of duke, through his German mother, from her uncle, the Duke of Dalberg, Prince Primate of Germany, but his deep respect for his father had prevented him from taking precedence as duke, till, at a later period, the Count himself insisted on his doing so, when a decree signed by the Emperor authorized the Comte Charles de Tascher de la Pagerie to bear henceforward the title of duke.

To prevent confusion, I shall at once use the title, although chronologically it was not yet adopted.

The principal functionaries had apartments in the palace. These were furnished with a somewhat bare and dreary magnificence; the rooms looked stately, but empty and uncomfortable, and many small articles of modern upholstery had to be purchased by the occupants, to adapt the majestic historical abode to the habits of the day.

CHAPTER II

My position at the Tuileries — The family de Tascher de la Pagerie — First opportunities of seeing the Empress — Her wonderful beauty — The color of her hair — An evening with the Empress in her private circle — Unseasonable interruption — Etiquette and its annoyances — Court obligations — Gilded chains.

THREE years had elapsed since the arrival of the family at the Tuileries, when I was informed that the future Duchesse de Tascher de la Pagerie wished to meet with a lady, born a gentlewoman, accustomed to good society, conscientious and reliable, who would be capable of entirely filling her place by her daughters, and who would constantly be their friend and guide. She would be "governess," only in the court sense of the function; not as a mere teacher, but as "governing" their education, superintending their studies, directing their reading, and accompanying them wherever they went. The German lady who had begun their education was about to be married, and the elder daughter being now sixteen, it was thought desirable to make a new choice, with a few modifications as to requirements. Some of my friends had thought of proposing me to fill this exceptional post.

The circumstance that members of my family were intimate with cousins of the de Tascher family would, it was considered, facilitate an introduction.

Finally, after much discussion, I was taken to the Tuileries, and presented to the Duchess. The sentinels and the servants in imperial livery had made me feel sufficiently nervous, but when I entered the private apartments occupied by the family, and, after passing through lugubrious dark passages, with lamps in mid-day, suddenly found myself in broad daylight, and within the rooms which, I was informed, would be mine if matters were favorably settled, my alarm increased to a painful degree. I felt that a new life, quite unknown, was opening before me, and its very brilliancy, to one who had always lived in retirement, was startling. My future pupils came forward to meet me: the elder, a blooming girl of sixteen, fresh as a rose, but more womanly in appearance than I expected, and with the graceful ease of manner which indicates the habit of general society; the younger, a pretty child of eleven, more shy than her sister. The rooms, plainly furnished in bright chintz, looked comfortable and homelike.

After a few minutes of general conversation, the door suddenly opened, and the Duchess came in quickly; a tall, graceful figure, very commanding in appearance, the court lady from head to foot, very beautiful, and most elegantly dressed. Being very near-sighted, she drew close to me with half-shut eyes, and peered down at me, very much as if she were trying to find a fly on the carpet; but in the conversation that followed, when we had resumed our seats, her manner was most courteous, and even a little embarrassed, through the evident fear of giving offense by expressing her wishes too plainly. Altogether, she left upon me the full impression of that considerate good breeding which is generally, but not always, the characteristic of distinguished rank.

I remained, however, for some days in doubt as to my final acceptance, being told by my friends that although everything had been found very satisfactory, there was some hesitation on account of my youth, the position being one of absolute trust, which was thought to require the experience of riper years. However, other applicants, though older than myself, seemed to present fewer guarantees; I was therefore finally engaged, and I hope I may be permitted to add that the decision never caused any regret.

It was late in the afternoon when, on the appointed day, I entered the palace, where I was fated to reside for nine years, during the most prosperous time of the Second Empire; but as yet all was unknown,—therefore necessarily uncertain,—and the nervous anxiety that I could not repress, though only natural under the circumstances, was a very disagreeable beginning. Some married daughters of the Comte de Tascher, with their children, were on a visit to their father, and the whole party came to my

apartments soon after my arrival, escorted by the
Duchess, who introduced me. They encouraged me
with so much unaffected good-nature and friendli-
ness, that I felt somewhat comforted, but fully recognized the truth of their parting remark, as they
went off laughingly: "You will feel happier a week
hence." As they left me, I was told to dress quickly,
as "mon père" had military habits, and was merci-
lessly punctual; so, giving my keys to the confidential maid sent to assist me, I begged her to select
what I ought to wear, hastily changing my attire
according to her instructions. A fresh ordeal now
awaited me: presentation to the Comtesse de Tascher, Princess Amélie von der Leyen, the "Durchlaucht" or Serene Highness, as the German servants
always called her. My pupils came to fetch me,
leading the way down a dark, narrow, winding staircase, then through a wide passage paved in white
and black marble, and through folding-doors, which
my eldest pupil opened, drawing back courteously
to leave me full precedence. I then entered a large,
handsome room hung round with pictures, and
richly furnished, where stood a group of ladies elegantly dressed; one of them, the Duchess, came
forward immediately, and led me to a dignified
elderly lady seated in a deep window, whose features
at once reminded me vividly of all the historical
portraits of German princesses I had seen in picture-galleries. Next, I made my obeisance to her
husband, General Comte de Tascher de la Pagerie,

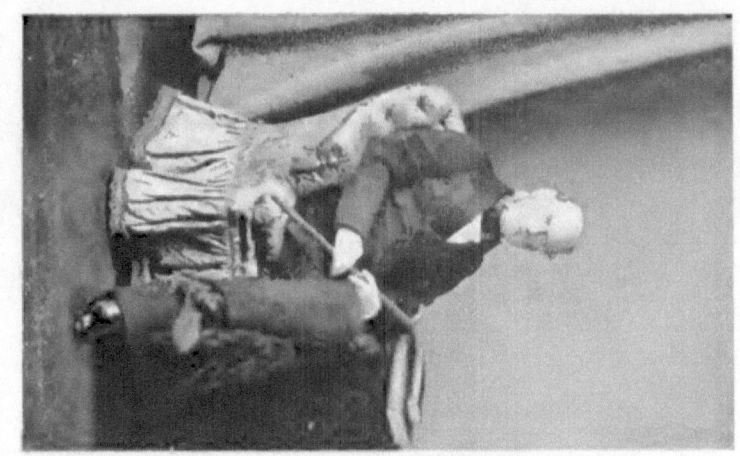

GENERAL, COMTE DE TASCHER DE LA PAGERIE.
FROM A PHOTOGRAPH BY LEVITSKY.

PRINCESS AMÉLIE VON DER LEYEN, COMTESSE DE TASCHER DE LA PAGERIE.
FROM A PHOTOGRAPH BY LEVITSKY.

DUC DE TASCHER.
FROM A PHOTOGRAPH BY BRAUN CLÉMENT & CO.

one of the most distinguished men in appearance that I had ever seen, whose eagle eye and aquiline profile recalled the Duke of Wellington. There was no time for conversation, the folding-doors being thrown open and dinner announced.

The large, handsome dining-room, where the numerous members of the family took their seats, the servants, in and out of livery, the display of plate, and all the ceremony of a formal dinner party, although no strangers were present, made me feel more than ever like a poor little sparrow which had strayed alone into an aviary of tropical birds. Conversation was general and very animated. I was seated next the (Princesse) Comtesse de Tascher, who from time to time spoke to me kindly, and urged me to partake of the dishes handed round. When the dinner was concluded, every one rose and moved to the door, where they stood in two lines, while the "Durchlaucht" passed out first, the others following her in couples, my pupils coming last. I was then allowed to retire for this first evening, and was thankful to do so after taking leave of the visitors, who were returning to Germany by the night train.

The next morning, of course, I found the family much reduced in number, when I went down to the *déjeuner*, or luncheon, and although the same stateliness was observed in the arrangements, everything looked less formidable. The Countess asked me kindly, "Are you less afraid of us, now?" and the Count, with smiling benevolence, inquired if my first night at the Tuileries had brought pleasant dreams? The Duke was "de service," or "in waiting," so I scarcely saw him, but he too welcomed me cordially, telling me "not to spoil his girls."

After luncheon, my two pupils and their brother, then a schoolboy of fifteen,[1] led me through the various rooms, pointing out the historical portraits of the Bonapartes and Beauharnais; those of the princes and princesses allied to their family; the portrait of their great-grandmother, the unfortunate Princess von der Leyen, and the flowers which she had worn at the fatal ball; also the portrait of the Prince-Primate of Germany, Duke of Dalberg, from whom their father inherited his title; and proudly explained the privilege of the Dalbergs, to be dubbed knights at the coronation of the emperors of Germany, when the herald called three times: "Ist kein Dalberg da?" ("Is there no Dalberg here?")

Then they showed me many treasures kept in handsome cabinets. One interested me particularly, a large plain gold ring containing the hair of Marie Antoinette, a thick lock of lovely golden hair, braided into a close plait; not the rich auburn hue of the Empress Eugénie, but a sweeter, paler color, usually seen only in childhood.

We then returned to our apartments, where the day was spent in putting all that I had brought

[1] Now Duc de Tascher de la Pagerie, and head of the family.

with me in due order; and the evening at the opera, whither I accompanied the Comtesse Stéphanie, an unmarried sister of the Duke, who lived at the Tuileries. We went in one of the Emperor's carriages, with coachman and groom in imperial livery, for which the police made room when needful. "Livrée de l'Empereur!" sufficed to cut through all files of carriages, and to pass everywhere, when proclaimed by the coachman in sonorous tones. We were conducted to the box, called "de service," devoted to the household, passing before bowing officials, and much stared at by spectators.

The next day was Sunday, with mass in the imperial chapel; but on the Monday I began fully the duties of my position, which I soon found was no sinecure, though made as pleasant as possible by the friendly kindness and courtesy of all around me. But from the moment when I was awakened in the morning till a late hour at night there was not an interval of time to breathe. The two girls being of different ages, the professors, classes, lectures, etc., were also totally different; so my days were spent in rushing out with one, and then rushing back to take the other somewhere else; on foot, in all weathers, which the Duchess considered necessary for the health of my pupils; but, as I had two, the fatigue was doubled. During these lectures, etc., I had to take notes incessantly, and to prepare the work for them. Often I was obliged to dress in ten minutes for a large dinner-party, because some professor had prolonged his lesson to the very last moment. The constant mental strain, added to the physical fatigue, was almost more than I could endure, and my health suffered so severely that I greatly feared the impossibility of continuing such an arduous task. In the evening there were dancing lessons three times a week; one at the English embassy, from which we returned at a late hour, and two others at the Tuileries in the apartments of the Duchesse de Bassano, our next neighbor. On the remaining evenings I frequently accompanied the (Princess) Countess, or the Comtesse Stéphanie, to theaters or operas, which, though very agreeable, added considerably to the overwhelming fatigue of the day. As to my own private correspondence, I was obliged to write necessary letters often very late at night, to the great anger of the Duchess, who rightly declared that I was wearing myself out; but I had no other resource. As time went on, matters happily became more easy, and after the marriage of my eldest pupil with Prince Maximilian von Thurn und Taxis, my task was considerably diminished. The work of the first year, however, was absolutely crushing.

I had seen the Empress Eugénie pass by in her carriage more than once, before I entered the Tuileries; but although I could not but think her beautiful, still, like most of those who saw her only under such circumstances, I had no idea of her real attractions. A few days after my arrival at the palace, as

I was crossing the large courtyard with the future Princess von Thurn und Taxis, I suddenly saw her stop short and perform the court courtesy,—a downward plunge, instead of the usual bend,—while the sentinel presented arms, as she hastily whispered: "L'Impératrice!"

There was the Empress standing before us, at a large window on the ground floor, an ideal vision robed in pale blue silk; the sun, forming a sort of halo around her, rested on her hair, which seemed all molten gold. I was absolutely startled, and my impression was that I had never seen such a beautiful creature, fully understanding at that moment the enthusiasm which I had supposed to be exaggerated. Her face was beaming with smiles as she recognized my pupil, nodding to her with the most unpretending good-nature. I remarked, after we had passed on, that I had supposed her hair to be of a darker hue, on which I was told to wait, before judging, till I had seen her in the shade instead of the sun.

I soon had an opportunity of seeing her in the chapel, as she passed before me on her way to the imperial gallery, bare-headed, as was her custom when not in the lower part of the building, where she condescended to wear a bonnet; but in the gallery she wore nothing on her hair, which now looked a dark, rich chestnut color, instead of the golden shade, like ripe wheat, which I had seen before. The habit which the Empress had adopted, of wearing no covering on her head during the Sunday high mass, was a sore grievance to the clergy, who in vain quoted the instructions of St. Paul addressed to women. But she listened to no remonstrance—as, indeed, was usually the case when anything suited her fancy or her convenience.

The opportunities of seeing the Empress were of almost daily occurrence, when she was at the Tuileries; for although we inhabited another part of the palace, she passed before our windows in her carriage when she went out for her habitual drives, and in the lower part of the chapel we were placed very near to her seat. The unfortunate Archbishop of Paris, who was shot during the Commune, usually attended the imperial mass, and was so near to me that the gold tassels of his vestment rested upon the desk of the pew where I knelt, with my pupils and Mesdemoiselles de Bassano. The Empress, who was just before us, with the Emperor (and at a later period, the Prince Imperial), never forgot, as she rose from her knees to go down the aisle, to turn toward our group with a gracious smile and bend; the deep courtesy, in reply, was not easy to perform in the narrow space allotted to us.

The first time that I was able to see the Empress in private life was at St. Cloud, where the de Tascher family occupied a villa adjoining the palace, with an entrance to the private grounds, of which we had a key.

One evening I had taken a drive with the Duchess,

and on our return she had gone into the garden
with her eldest daughter, to enjoy the fresh air, re-
questing me to order the lamps for the drawing-
room. I had just laid my hand on the bell, when I
heard a voice asking for the Duchess, and the door
suddenly opening, I saw a lady standing in the entrance. Supposing her to be a visitor from Paris,
I immediately went toward her, begging her to
come in while I called the Duchess, who was in the
garden; but I saw some hesitation, and, although
the room was nearly dark, a ray of moonlight resting
on her face revealed the Empress Eugénie. I was
startled, and hardly knew what I ought to do, paus-
ing for a moment, on which she hastily took flight,
closing the door. I ran to the Duchess: "Madame," I
said, "the Empress is here!" She hastily came forward,
while the door opened again, but this time the Empress was accompanied by the Duc de Tascher and a
numerous suite, as she came in quickly, with extended hands, which the Duchess kissed. She had
previously run on alone, leaving the others behind
her, and in the anteroom had asked the servant on
duty if the Duchess was at home, wishing to surprise
her. The man, who was half asleep, sprang to his
feet with evident trepidation; on seeing which she
exclaimed: "Do you know me?" "Certainly—I
have the honor of knowing your Majesty." "Oh!
how tiresome!" she cried ("*Comme c'est ennuyeux!*");
"everybody knows me!" She hastily opened the
door before her, and saw that I too recognized her;

on which she flew to the Duke, saying, "Tascher! Tascher! I cannot go in—there is a strange lady!" He answered, laughing, that he thought he knew who that strange lady must be, and that Her Majesty need not be alarmed, on which she consented to return. As the Duchess welcomed her warmly, she said that she had felt quite shy ("intimidée") when she saw "madame",—with a smiling bend toward me,—on which I was presented in due form to her very gracious Majesty. The whole party then went on the terrace before the house, and, after assisting in providing seats, I withdrew, fearing to intrude on their privacy. But in a few minutes my pupil came running in; the Empress had asked why I had retired, and had expressed a particular wish that I should join them. It was rather an ordeal to go through, when I found myself standing at the top of a flight of steps, which I had to descend in full view of the large court circle before me; the more so as there was bright moonlight, and I knew that I must remain standing till permission was given to sit down. But the Empress saw me immediately, and with her usual grace of manner desired me to be seated, using her habitual polite circumlocution — "Will you not sit down?" I obeyed, with the requisite low courtesy, and a most pleasant evening followed, the Empress chatting gaily and familiarly, as she energetically dug up the gravel at her feet with a tall walking-stick which she held in her hand, repeatedly addressing me personally, with marked affability. When an opportunity occurred, she called me to her side, and gave me a chair with her own hand. In short, it was impossible to show more kindness and consideration than I noticed toward every one present.

She spoke French with a marked Spanish accent, and to my surprise her voice had the harsh guttural sounds so frequent among Castilians, but which seemed strangely foreign to that sweet face, so delicate in its loveliness.

My feminine readers will perhaps wish to know "how she was dressed" on this occasion, and I can only answer, "As simply as possible." She wore a dress of a soft gray summer stuff, over a striped blue and white silk underskirt; a loose mantle of the same pale gray was thrown over all. She held a tall walking-stick in her hand, and wore a straw hat of the Tyrolese shape, with a Tyrolese plume of black and white feathers.

The Duchess offered tea, which was accepted, and the whole party adjourned to the villa, where it was immediately served. The Empress was in high spirits, laughing and talking merrily, and seeming thoroughly to enjoy her escape from her usual trammels, when to the consternation of her hostess, and her own very evident annoyance, the door opened, and a lady, inhabiting a neighboring villa, sailed in, followed by her daughter, both in full toilet. She held a high post at court, but nothing on this occasion called for her presence, which was flagrantly intrusive. She explained that she had heard the voices in the garden, and begged "to be allowed a share in the good fortune of her neighbors." A chill had fallen on the whole party; the Empress, suddenly silent and cold, played with her tea-spoon, looking grave and displeased, while the intruder talked of her "beautiful dahlias," which she wished so much to show to Her Majesty — at nearly eleven o'clock at night! It was so near; would not Her Majesty stop on her way back to the palace, and see the dahlias?

The Empress evidently wished particularly to be let alone; but at last she rose with an air of weary resignation: "Well! let us go and see the dahlias!"

The pleasant evening was over, and the momentary freedom which had made it so agreeable was cut short, merely because one court lady was determined to enjoy the same mark of favor that had been bestowed on another court lady.

It is said that in the early years of her reign Queen Victoria exclaimed: "What is the use of being a queen, if one cannot do as one likes?" She soon was obliged to learn that, of all women, queens are those who least do as they like. The Empress Eugénie had wished to enjoy royal honors, and she, too, had to learn that an amount of restraint for which she was ill prepared by a life of absolute liberty must be the necessary consequence of her high position. Etiquette, though much modernized, and consequently made less irksome than it was in the days of poor Marie Antoinette, yet still stood in her way on every side. She could not risk giving offense, and she must court popularity. The bird which had always flown freely wherever the wish of the hour guided its flight was now in a gilded cage, tied down by silken links as difficult to break as iron chains.

She would have wished to walk about freely, without state or ceremony, except on official occasions, when she did not dislike playing the part of Empress; but she could not leave the palace without a numerous suite, in a carriage and four with outriders; nor get rid of the necessity of incessantly bowing to the spectators, which she performed both graciously and gracefully, but with unavoidable weariness. She had twelve ladies-in-waiting, some of whom were her personal friends; others had been chosen for political reasons, and she did not particularly care for them; but she could show no preference. Two ladies at a time were in waiting,—in Paris, for a week, at the country residences, for a month. Each lady, in turn, was "de grand service," as it was called, or in full waiting; that is, she had a right to go with the Empress in her carriage, and take precedence on all occasions, while the other followed in the second carriage, with the chamberlain in waiting. The next day matters were reversed, and the other lady was "de grand service," whether or not the Empress liked the change.

In all matters she was subjected to perpetual constraint, and forced to play an artificial part extremely trying to one not born in the purple, and of a particularly frank, straightforward disposition. Those who knew her as Mademoiselle de Montijo, and had an opportunity of observing her extreme independence of character, openly declared that she would never submit to court trammels, and would suddenly break through them in some very apparent manner. She did not break through them, and she endured for many years her gilded chains; but that she felt their weight severely is undeniable, and she certainly found out that her fairy-land did not mean a paradise.

CHAPTER III

Regulations of the palace — The detectives — Inconveniences of the palace — The painting-room of Mademoiselle Hortense de Tascher — Pasini, the artist — Apartments of the Empress — View on the garden of the Tuileries — What it was then — Description of the various rooms — Audiences granted by the Empress — High mass on Sundays — The Emperor's demeanor — The sermon — Etiquette — The wardrobe regions above the apartments of the Empress — "Pepa," the Empress's Spanish maid — The jailer's daughters — Anecdote of the Emperor — The privy-purse of the Empress.

ALL the inmates of the palace of every rank were subjected to a sort of military discipline. The gates, always guarded by sentinels, were closed at midnight; any one returning after that hour was noted by the officer in command, and reported the next morning. Every day the picket of guards was changed, and a fresh password was given.

Shortly after my arrival at the Tuileries I had gone to an evening party, with the permission of the Duchess, escorted by some friends, who brought me back after the fatal hour — of which, as yet, I did not know the rule. The next morning I was much teased, good-humoredly, by the Duc de Tascher as to my delinquencies; I had been "reported to him as having returned after the gates had been closed," and he looked very solemn.

I was a good deal startled, pleading the permission of the Duchess, and the safety of my escort; but after having sufficiently enjoyed my alarm he laughed, and explained that it was a general rule to keep the heads of the different private households informed of the doings of all those inhabiting their quarters in the palace; but that I might safely commit the offense again, under the same circumstances. There was, however, so much trouble and ceremony attending the opening of the gates, after any such Cinderella mishap, that I soon gave up all evening parties in case I could not be sure of returning before the fatal hour.

Besides the military guards of the palace, there was a strong force of detectives always standing about the principal doors, in groups, conversing together carelessly, with an assumed indifference, while their sharp eyes watched keenly all those who came and went. Every inmate of the palace was, of course, well known to these men, who were dressed to look as much like ordinary gentlemen as they could, although the practised eye quickly recognized the scowling, sinister glance, and a sort of disreputable look, which made the contact of these men what the Scotch would call "uncanny." The ladies of the palace were often surprised to receive bows in the street from unknown persons, who also would often spring forward to help them in any difficulty; on such occasions the rule was to receive their advances most graciously. They were not men whom it would have been prudent to offend in any way by misplaced haughtiness, and it was often really convenient to hear from some stranger the authoritative and unexpected: "Laissez passer madame," when an uninitiated ordinary policeman, or sentinel, was troublesome.

The Duc de Tascher kindly took me over the apartments, shortly after my arrival at the palace. It must be acknowledged that the Tuileries, built at different periods, and arranged for various necessities, was not a convenient residence. Several of the large galleries had been cut up into apartments for the use of the numerous members of Louis Philippe's family; they were separated by passages having no means of external light or ventilation, so that lamps burned day and night, and the air was close and heavy. The different floors communicated in the interior by narrow winding staircases, also lighted at all times; so that the first impression to visitors was strangely lugubrious and funereal. Two floors had also been often made out of one; so that in such cases the ceilings were low, and the deep windows prevented the free transmission of light, especially darkening the rooms toward the north, looking on the rue de Rivoli. The conveniences of modern life were very imperfect. During the greater part of the Emperor's reign, there was not even water put in, and the daily supply of the inmates was brought up in pails to the various apartments. The sanitary arrangements and drainage were very bad; in the upper regions inhabited by the servants the air was absolutely pestilential, as I was able to judge several times a week; for we had to cross them before reaching the painting-room where Mademoiselle Hortense de Tascher took lessons, given to her regularly for many years by the well-known artist Pasini, for whom we all felt great esteem and warm friendship.

Pasini, when I first knew him, was a young and still struggling artist just returned from Persia, whither he had followed the French Legation, having been engaged by the minister, Monsieur Bourée, to take sketches of the country. It was there that his studies developed his peculiar appreciation and admirable interpretation of Oriental scenery, which have now given him fame and fortune; but he was as yet little known, and we were enabled to follow his rising career, step by step, with deep interest, and ever-increasing esteem for his private character as well as for his artistic talent.

The Empress occupied the first floor, looking toward the garden, so beautiful then with its groves of horse-chestnut-trees—now, alas! partially cut down and replanted, since the ravages committed during the siege and the Commune. In those days the foliage of the splendid old trees formed an

EMPRESS EUGÉNIE WEARING A SPANISH MANTILLA.
ENGRAVED BY R. G. TIETZE, FROM A PHOTOGRAPH BY BRAUN, CLÉMENT & CO.

impenetrable canopy overhead, and the great central avenue leading to the Champs-Élysées, with the Arc de Triomphe in the distance, was bordered in May by a gigantic wall of blossoms on each side. It is impossible, at the present time, to form any idea of what the garden was then, with the splendid palace in the background, the walks bordered by orange-trees with their sweet perfume, the well-kept parterres, the terraces, the statues, and the elegantly dressed crowd listening to the military band.

The Empress's apartments comprised ten rooms, communicating by a small private staircase with the Emperor's, which were on the ground floor, near those afterward devoted to the use of the Prince Imperial. In the first years of the Empire the furniture of the private apartments was not remarkable; but at a later period the rooms used by the Empress were arranged with exquisite taste and elegance.

The first salon, decorated in two shades of pale green with gold tracings and moldings, contained an immense mirror, which reflected the whole view of the gardens, and of the Champs-Élysées, as far as the Arc de l'Étoile. Above the doors were painted tropical birds with bright plumage. This delightful and charming room, called the Salon Vert, was used by the chamberlains and ladies-in-waiting. It opened into the Salon Rose, decorated in different shades of rose-color. The chimneypiece was of white marble adorned with lapis lazuli and gold; the doors were decorated with paintings of flowers; the ceiling, painted by Chaplin, represented the Arts paying homage to the Empress, and a genius carrying the Prince Imperial in the midst of flowers.

It was there that visitors admitted to the honor of a private audience awaited Her Majesty's pleasure. Thence they were ushered into the Salon Bleu, which was adorned with medallion portraits of the Duchesses de Cadore, de Persigny, de Morny, de Malakoff, the Princesse Anna Murat (afterwards Duchesse de Mouchy), and the Comtesse Walewska. Here, surrounded by flowers and rare gems of art, the Empress received her guests with such grace and kindness that all felt immediately at home, and formality soon disappeared. The only trying moment was that of taking leave, etiquette forbidding visitors to retire till a gesture, or a gracious bend of the head, authorized them to do so, while the good-nature of the Empress, shrinking from what seemed an unkind proceeding, often prolonged the interview to an extent which was embarrassing on both sides.

Beyond the Salon Bleu was the private room of the Empress, with a large writing-table for her use, opposite to which, when I saw it, hung a portrait of the Prince Imperial as an infant, wearing the broad red ribbon of the Legion of Honor on his little white frock. About the walls, in glazed cabinets, were autographs, manuscripts, and various historical relics. But the description of one period may not apply to another, as the Empress was fond of making changes in the arrangements of her apartments.

A small boudoir, protected against drafts by a folding-screen with glass panels, divided this room from a library surrounded with book-cases of ebony and gold.

Then came a large dressing-room, an oratory in which was an altar concealed by folding doors, opened for the celebration of the mass, but habitually closed; and beyond, the large and magnificent bed-room of the Empress.

During the first years of the Empire, when she performed her private devotions, she went to the chapel, which was then closed; for she particularly disliked to be observed or watched at that time. At a later period, the above-mentioned oratory was arranged so as to enable her to attend mass without leaving her apartments.

But on Sundays, immediately after the déjeuner or luncheon, there was high mass, which the Emperor and Empress attended with some ceremonial, accompanied by the "service d'honneur," the gentlemen in full court uniform, the ladies in elegant morning dresses. On ordinary Sundays the royal party were in a gallery facing the altar; but on particular occasions, and during the whole of Lent, they came into the lower part of the chapel, where arm-chairs covered with crimson velvet, each having its "prie-dieu" and cushions before it, were prepared for the Emperor and Empress, who were received in state by the clergy at the door, when the deep-voiced official announced in a loud tone:

"L'Empereur!"

The Emperor always wore the uniform of a general, with the ribbon of the Legion of Honor; the Empress, exquisitely dressed, moved by his side with a grace and dignity which none present could forget. The Emperor's grave countenance and manner impressed the bystanders with a sort of awe; but his figure was ungainly and ill-proportioned, and his swaying gait was unpleasing.

In France, where men affect a sort of indifference in religious matters (when not positively hostile), it is their general habit to remain standing during the services when women kneel.

Napoleon III. never adopted this custom; he always knelt and remained kneeling at all the portions of the service where it is required. Whatever may have been his real feelings of religious fervor, his demeanor was certainly perfectly reverent, and he had every appearance of following the service with all due respect.

The sermon, to the great annoyance of the preachers, was timed to last exactly half an hour, and began immediately after the gospel of the mass, when the gentlemen in attendance turned the chairs of the Emperor and Empress so as to place them exactly in front of the pulpit. The preacher began his address with a low bow, saying: "Sire — Madame," instead of the usual "Mes frères." The Emperor sat motionless, his clasped hands before him; but his peculiar habit of incessantly twirling his thumbs often disconcerted the preacher, who was further disquieted by the limited time granted to him, and by the presence of an official, who stepped forward and stood before the altar as a warning to conclude the discourse, which was often wound up with evident haste.

The imperial chairs were then turned toward the altar, and the service continued with exquisite singing and a seemingly angelic accompaniment of harps. When the little Prince was old enough to go to church he had a seat next to his father, who often stooped down to show him the places in his book. He always behaved with exemplary gravity, and looked very pretty in his black velvet suit, with red stockings and a large lace collar, like a young cavalier of the olden time.

After mass was over, the Emperor and Empress passed out with the same state as when coming in; but on leaving the chapel, the Emperor spoke to officers of different regiments, who usually stood in the adjoining *salle*, or hall, and the Empress retired to her apartments, where she gave audience in the "Salon Bleu" to those who had obtained that favor.

Above the apartments of the Empress, in one of the half-floors previously alluded to, was the dwelling of "Pepa," the former Spanish maid of Mademoiselle de Montijo; she had begun life very humbly as an ordinary servant, and was now entitled "treasurer" to the Empress, having the care of her jewels and wardrobe. "Pepa" was principally assisted by two young ladies, who had been well educated at the school of the Legion of Honor of St. Denis, and were far superior to her in intelligence and manners. They were the daughters of the jailer at Ham, the fortress where Louis Napoleon was imprisoned for six years, after his attempt at Boulogne, under Louis Philippe. The jailer had filled his unpleasant mission with respect and consideration for the future Emperor, who never forgot any kindness shown to him, and who immediately remembered the two young women, when the household of the Empress was appointed on her marriage. The governor of the fortress had been, of course, in an unpleasant position after the flight of the prisoner, for whom he was responsible, much to the alarm of his wife, who lamented over the "ingratitude" of the fugitive.

"How could he play us such a trick," she said "after all our kindness to him? I always sent him such excellent broth!"

When the former prisoner became Emperor of the French, he sent for the governor of Ham and his wife, who both came into his presence with some trepidation. The Emperor, with his usual graceful affability, then said that, having experienced the watchful care of his person shown by the governor during his imprisonment, he felt full confidence as to the manner in which he would be guarded by him in future, and consequently begged that he would accept the post of governor of the St. Cloud palace.

Then turning to the governor's wife, he added, with a smile, that he hoped she would no longer consider that her good broth had been wasted.

The position secured for the jailer's daughters ought to have been a good one for young women of their rank in life; but the ill-temper and jealousy of "Pepa" greatly destroyed their peace, and quarrels were frequent in the wardrobe regions. "Pepa" had married an officer in an infantry regiment, and was henceforth entitled "Madame Pollet"; but she was nevertheless best known in the household as "Pepa," and was as much hated under one denomination as under the other. She was persistently supported by the Empress, who would hear nothing against her, although the manner in which "Pepa" levied blackmail on all the tradespeople employed by the Empress, and the bribes which she received on all sides from those who hoped to secure her influence, and consequently tried to propitiate her, constituted a scandalous state of affairs, which greatly displeased the Emperor when any instances came to his knowledge. In fact, beyond her especial attributions, the Empress did not listen to any direct interference from "Pepa," or allow her to act ostensibly as protectress to any one; but that she had over her mistress the sort of influence which a confidential maid easily acquires was evident from the deference shown to her by the ladies of the palace, who seemed greatly to fear any hostility on her part.

The region over which her particular authority was exercised comprised several rooms, entirely surrounded by wardrobes in plain oak, with sliding panels, in which all the various articles of clothing were arranged in perfect order. Four lay-figures, exactly measured to fit the dresses worn by the Empress, were used to diminish the necessity of too much trying on, and also to prepare her toilet for the day. Orders were given through a speaking-pipe in the dressing-room, and the figure came down on a sort of lift through an opening in the ceiling, dressed in all that the Empress was about to wear. The object of this arrangement was to save time, and also to avoid the necessity of crushing the voluminous dresses of the period in the narrow back-staircases.

The Empress had a privy purse of 1,200,000 francs a year ($240,000); of this large sum, 100,000 francs ($20,000) were devoted to her toilet; the rest was chiefly employed in gifts and charities. It was said at that time that a portion was invested; this has been denied since, although extremely probable, and certainly very justifiable.

NAPOLEON III. AND THE EMPRESS EUGÉNIE.

Twice a year a certain number of her dresses were discarded, and divided between "Pepa" and the other two maids, the former having half. This was extremely profitable, as even the lace trimmings were not removed—with the exception of the broad and very valuable lace, which was of course preserved and transferred from one dress to another. I remember seeing "Pepa" in full toilet (probably one inherited from the Empress), but looking unmistakably plebeian; a small, dark, bony woman of very Spanish type, her large hands in white gloves. She spoke horrible French, and was evidently a very ordinary person in every respect. She followed the Empress to England after the fall of the Empire, but died shortly afterward, leaving a comfortable fortune to her heirs.

CHAPTER IV

Daily life of the Court — Duties of the ladies-in-waiting — Charities of the Emperor and Empress — The Prince Imperial — Drives of the Empress — A rheumatic chamberlain — The evenings at the Court — Dinner — The "service d'honneur" — Etiquette — Habitual simplicity of the Empress in her morning-dress — Her usual evening toilet — The mechanical piano — Sudden wish of the Empress to dance the "Lancers" — Mademoiselle de Taseher summoned to teach the figures — Difficulties caused by petty court jealousies — Late hours of the Empress — Anecdote of the Emperor — His amiable disposition in private life — Impulsive nature of the Empress.

"PEPA and her assistants," of course, lived at the palace, but the ladies-in-waiting did not sleep at the Tuileries when the court was in Paris. They were fetched, in a carriage devoted to their use, for their hours of duty, which began at two o'clock in the afternoon. They awaited her Majesty's pleasure in the "Salon Vert," where the "service d'honneur" assembled, and where the ladies kept their books, writing-materials, and needlework. After their usual drive with the Empress, they were taken to their homes for their evening toilet; and returned to the palace in full dress for the dinner, which was served at half-past seven. The déjeuner, or midday meal, was at half-past eleven; in Paris, the Emperor and Empress partook of it alone till the Prince Imperial was old enough to join them; but at the country residences the "service d'honneur" was admitted to both meals, with, also, the guests staying there on a visit. After the "déjeuner," the Emperor usually followed the Empress to her private room, where the little Prince was brought, and where they enjoyed family life like ordinary mortals, for a short respite. The Empress then admitted her private secretary, and examined with him the innumerable petitions received daily. Both the Emperor and Empress were generous in their charities—the Emperor even to excess; it has been stated that his various gifts and grants amounted to a daily sum of 10,000 francs ($2000).

When the time came for the daily drive, the ladies and the "service d'honneur" in general were summoned to attend the Empress, who went out in an open carriage and four, with postilions and outriders in green and gold liveries; an equerry rode by the carriage-door. She was always smiling, graciously bowing, and invariably putting on a pair of apparently tight-fitting new gloves, a slight dereliction from imperial etiquette, which was often remarked. The lady-in-waiting who was "de grand service" sat by her side in the carriage; a second carriage followed with another lady and a chamberlain. My young charges always ran to the window when the drums beat the salute, and if the chamberlain in the second carriage was busily engaged in gathering wraps around him, they exclaimed, laughing: "There is papa!" for the Duc de Tascher, being very rheumatic, particularly disliked the open carriages in winter weather.

The young Prince Imperial, attended by his governess, and afterward by his tutor, was always accompanied by a military escort, which was considered necessary for his safety; but all hearts warmed to the pretty boy, who so gracefully raised his little cap and smiled so confidingly and so happily. The Parisians, even those of the lowest orders, still speak with affection and regret of "le petit Prince."

The dinner was served in the "Salon de Louis XIV."; but the "service d'honneur" assembled in the "Salon d'Apollon" (where the evenings were habitually spent), to await the Emperor and Empress, who came in together. When the silent bend of an official announced that all was ready, the Emperor gave his arm to the Empress, and both, passing out first, took their seats at the center of the dinner-table, side by side, the others following, according to rank and precedence. The gentlemen wore either their uniforms or the court-dress, which differed but little from the ordinary evening coat, but with a lining of white moiré silk. The ladies wore low-made evening dress; but there was greater indulgence on the part of the kind imperial hosts than is usually found in courts; if really needful, in consequence of indisposition, a *pèlerine* of white quilted satin and sleeves of the same were tolerated as a protection for the shoulders and arms. The Empress usually wore velvet of rich, dark colors, which was particularly becoming to her exquisitely fair complexion. The Emperor liked to see her richly dressed, and often objected to the extreme simplicity of her morning attire, which, it must be acknowledged, was often too fanciful to be appropriate to her high position. Everything she wore was well made, and perfectly neat; her hair was beautifully dressed; but, for instance, she liked the comfort of loose garibaldi bodices of red flannel, with a plain black silk skirt, over a red flannel underskirt; all of which was concealed, when she went out, by a handsome cloak and the fur-coverings of the open carriages. I have seen her wear, within the palace, a tight jacket of knitted black wool, with a gray border, over the silk and crape dress which she wore as second mourning for her sister, the Duchess of Alva. It was a sort of wrap which one would expect to see on the shoulders of some old crone bending over her fire, rather than on the graceful figure of the beautiful Empress of the French. I might quote other instances—such as her wearing a loose jacket of a small black and white check, in coarse woolen stuff bordered with red flannel.

After dinner the court adjourned to the splendid room called "Salon d'Apollon," where coffee was handed round; the Emperor took his cup standing, accompanied by cigarettes, which it was his habit to smoke incessantly. The ladies present remained standing till they were requested to sit down; but the Emperor's courtesy did not allow them to wait long before receiving the requisite authorization. The gentlemen, however, stood upright during the whole evening, and many found this a trial. The evenings were very heavy in general, a fact which those admitted to them did not attempt to conceal.

In the time of Louis Philippe, Queen Marie Amélie and the princesses, her daughters-in-law, sat round a table with needlework, which at least provided occupation; but during the Empire conversation was the principal resource, and this often flagged. The Emperor was benevolent but silent; the Empress tried to talk incessantly, with real or feigned vivacity; sometimes, in the young days of the Empire, she proposed dancing, and one of the gentlemen present turned the handle of a mechanical piano, playing dancing tunes. I remember that one evening, shortly after my arrival at the palace, we were all seated quietly in the salon of the Duke's mother (Princesse) Comtesse de Tascher, after dinner, when suddenly the chamberlain-in-waiting appeared: the Empress wished to dance the "lancers" in vogue that winter, and nobody present knew the figures. It had been suggested that Mademoiselle de Tascher, who habitually attended the dancing lessons at the British Embassy, was probably initiated in the mysteries of the new dance — and she must come immediately to teach everybody. The Duchess, who was going to a private ball, protested vehemently that her daughter was a mere school-girl, not yet introduced into society; she was not dressed appropriately for such an unexpected honor; she could not go without her mother, etc. The chamberlain, with languid good breeding and perfect indifference, coolly answered:

"All I know is that she is to come immediately, and must not stop to dress; I suppose you may come too, if you like, but you must not keep her Majesty waiting." So the Duchess and her daughter followed the chamberlain, Mademoiselle de Tascher considerably vexed at having no time to change her dark-green silk dress for more becoming attire; but there was no help for it, and she must obey. She was warmly received by the Empress (dressed in crimson velvet and diamonds), gave the required lesson in the "lancers," danced with the Emperor, who broke her fan, and apologized, while she, though a "school-girl," replied, in courtier-like phrase, that she was "too happy to have such a remembrance of His Majesty," who, unfortunately, forgot all about it the next day, and thus omitted to send her a more pleasant remembrance. At ten o'clock, according to custom, a tea-table was brought in, with a tray of cool drinks for those who preferred them. The Empress, in high spirits, made the tea herself, instead of leaving the matter to her ladies, and my "school-girl" greatly enjoyed the whole adventure.

The Empress would have liked to spend the evening sometimes with the de Tascher family, whose cheerfulness, as she said once in my presence, "would cure the jaundice"; but the question of petty court jealousies again stood in her way; she visited them, but only at long intervals, when some apparent reason justified the exception. Usually, after taking tea, the Emperor retired "to transact business with his private secretary," as was stated; what that "business" was, on too frequent occasions, had better not be too closely examined. The Empress usually remained till about half-past eleven, when she disappeared, and as the last fold of her train left the doorway, all the men present, who had been standing the whole evening, uttered a sigh of relief as they threw themselves on the sofas, with undisguised satisfaction.

The Duc de Tascher, who suffered from rheumatic gout, found this obligation of etiquette particularly trying, and being privileged in many respects, he frequently slipped into the next room, where he could sit down, and even indulge in a momentary doze, with impunity. Often, on returning from some theater with one of the ladies of the family, I met him coming, wearily, from the imperial quarters, and as he said "good night," he would add, with a groan: "There is no way of inducing the Empress to go to bed!" Her personal attendants could say much more on the subject, for even after retiring to her private apartments, she often lingered till the small hours of the night.

One evening, as the Duke afterward told me, he

GARDEN FRONT OF THE TUILERIES.

FROM A PHOTOGRAPH.

had escaped to the neighboring room, where he habitually took refuge, and was seated, writing a letter, when the Emperor suddenly came in. Of course, the Duke immediately sprang to his feet, but the Emperor good-humoredly desired him not to disturb himself, but to go on with his letter. On such occasions, the rule is to obey without any objection, the sovereign's will being considered paramount. The Duke, consequently, sat down and quietly continued his letter, though much discomfited by the presence of the Emperor, who paced the room to and fro, smoking his cigarette, and humming a tune. The Duke, however, leisurely finished and folded his letter, sealing it deliberately with the large official seal in red wax, and carefully adding the stamp of the Household. The Emperor then drew near:

"Have you finished, Tascher?"

"Yes, Sire."

"*Quite* finished?"

"Yes, Sire."

"Then—I may take the inkstand?"

The good-natured simplicity of the act was extremely characteristic. There never was a more amiable man in private life than the Emperor Napoleon III., or one more absolutely unpretending. His constant gentleness, his unvarying patient kindness, were only too much preyed upon by many of those around him; but he was certainly deeply loved by all who were in habitual personal contact with him: more loved than was the Empress Eugénie, notwith-

standing her personal charms. She was extremely
good-natured, thoroughly natural, devoid of haughtiness (a great merit in such a position), but impulsive
and hot-tempered; too sincere, too straightforward,
to conceal her varying impressions; withal, fanciful,
and tenacious in her fancies, which often irritated
those who had to yield to her wishes despite difficulties and inconvenience. "One of the Empress's
whims!" was often the comment of her attendants,
down to the domestic servants of the palace. The
Emperor, always quiet, and even apathetic, disturbed
no one; but if an appeal were made to his feelings,
he could not resist. There was a sort of tender-
hearted, sentimental softness in his nature, which
recalled the "sensibility" of bygone days; probably
inherited from his mother, Queen Hortense. This
often led him astray, and is the real explanation of
many errors. He was far from being deliberately
false, as has been so often asserted; but, unfortunately, he was more a man of feeling than a man of
principle. This led to weakness and vacillation;
though, like many others whose natures are too
yielding, when he had finally taken a decision, he
was firm, even to obstinacy. Any one more unlike
the blood-thirsty tyrant depicted by Victor Hugo
and other political adversaries, could scarcely be imagined. The sight of the battle-field of Solferino
had left on his mind such an impression of horror as
to destroy all dreams of military glory, and it was
with the greatest unwillingness that he was drawn

into the wars that followed, principally, alas! through
the pertinacious influence of the Empress Eugénie,
who had not seen a battle-field, and who only knew
the conventional pictures of glory and heroism, without their fearful cost.

The Empress was extremely agreeable and good-natured, but there was no softness in her character.
Even with regard to those dearest to her,—the Emperor and her son,—she was influenced more by a
chivalrous, romantic ideal, than by any natural tenderness. Her aim was to show herself a Roman wife
and mother, and this led her, on many occasions, to
a sort of apparent harshness, which caused her to be
misjudged.

CHAPTER V

The Emperor's drives — His opinion of mankind in general — The special police attached to the Emperor's person — Alessandri, the detective — The Orsini attempt on the Emperor's life — Impression at the Tuileries — The return of the Emperor and Empress — Letter from the Marquis of Waterford — My life at the Tuileries — Games of chess with the Archbishop of Bourges — Costume balls — Banquet on the marriage of Prince Napoleon with the Princess Clotilde of Savoy — The ball — A waltz of the Emperor with the Princess rendered impossible — Costume of the Empress.

THE Emperor usually went out in a phaëton or brake, which he drove himself, attended only by one gentleman, and two grooms in livery. When the peculiar beat of the drums announced the passage of any member of the imperial family, a crowd, always sprinkled with detectives, gathered before the gates, and as the drums beat the salute, "One, two — one, two, three — one, two — one, two, three," the Emperor passed out, slightly touching his hat, in acknowledgment of the cries of "Vive l'Empereur!" His face, especially during the last years of the Empire, was always grave and careworn, but impenetrable, and as expressionless as a mask.

The old Comte de Tascher de la Pagerie related that in the beginning of the Empire, when he was once driving out with the Emperor, he noticed, with great surprise, his cold, calm demeanor in the midst of the absolutely delirious enthusiasm with which he was greeted by the people; and using the freedom of his privileged position as a relation and an old friend, he expressed his astonishment that the Emperor seemed to feel so little moved or pleased at such a reception. The Emperor, with his calm smile, gravely answered: " It is because I know mankind, Tascher." (" C'est que je connais les hommes, Tascher.") The storm of abuse and calumny which followed his reverses proved how true was his appreciation of the real value of such demonstrations.

When the Emperor thus left the palace without any apparent state, an unpretending coupé or brougham was always seen to follow at a short distance; this contained the chief of the police attached to the Emperor's person, whose myrmidons were scattered along the way. There was one especially, a Corsican named Alessandri, who was devoted to the Emperor with a sort of canine fidelity, and was always near him when he went out; so that to the initiated the presence of Alessandri was symptomatic of the approach of the sovereign. He always paced the pavement before the Tuileries till the Emperor's phaëton came out, and daily we met him as we left the palace for our usual walk. I remember one very cold day going out with the Princess von Thurn und Taxis (who had been my eldest pupil); we were both wrapped in long cloaks falling to the ground and wore double veils, so that I said to the Princess: "We shall not be recognized to-day!" Scarcely had I spoken, when, as we stepped under the arcades of the Rue de Rivoli, we met Alessandri. One glance, and his hat was off, with a low bow. The acuteness of those men was wonderful.

It was Alessandri who arrested the would-be assassin, Pianori, and who disabled him by the ready use of his Corsican stiletto. It was Alessandri who, on the terrible night of the Orsini explosions, forcibly drew the Emperor and Empress from the shattered carriage in the midst of the darkness and confusion, the cries of the wounded, and the struggles of the fallen horses of the escort, crying:

"Sire, Madame, descendez!"

There was no time for ceremony; the strong hand of the faithful Corsican disengaged them from the wreck, and dragged them into the opera-house, where at least they were safe.

Many persons thoughtlessly criticized as unfeeling the presence of the imperial party at the opera after such a terrible catastrophe. But it should be remembered that the explosion had torn up the pavement, and extinguished the gas, and that there were many victims to be cared for, and many precautions to be taken before the Emperor and Empress could safely return to the imperial home, where on that eventful night all was anxiety and terror.

The Comte de Tascher was suffering from a bad

attack of gout, and after dinner we were all assembled in his room, when we heard the drums beating the imperial salute, and, going to the window, we saw the carriages with their large lamps at the four corners, and an escort of lancers. The Emperor and Empress were going to the opera, with the Duke of Saxe-Coburg, brother to Prince Albert, the consort of Queen Victoria. I remember feeling at the time one of those inexplicable misgivings which all have experienced; I disliked this announced gala evening at the opera, remembering historical examples of tragic events. But the impression was evanescent, and when we were dismissed, because the invalid wished to rest, Robert de Tascher came with his sisters to our rooms, and there we were spending a merry evening, when the Comtesse Stéphanie suddenly entered, pale as death.

"Something dreadful has happened—there has been an attempt on the Emperor's life—they are bringing back killed and wounded soldiers."

With one bound, Robert de Tascher was gone; he soon came back to say that the Emperor and Empress were uninjured, but there were many victims. Shells had been thrown, and the explosion had been terrific.

I immediately thought of the Duc de Tascher, who was not in waiting, and who had gone with the Duchesse to another theater. I suggested that he ought to be told immediately; Robert de Tascher thanked me for reminding him, and was off in a moment. The Duke, horrified at the news, went immediately to the opera, where he found the Emperor and Empress in the retiring-room behind the imperial box. The white satin dress of the Empress was stained with blood, but she seemed perfectly calm, as she extended her hand to him, saying gravely: "Well, Charles, you see what life is worth." The Emperor was far less calm than his wife; he seemed much excited and deeply moved. That night, one hundred and fifty-six victims had suffered for his sake, in the attempt to take his life, and the magnitude of the catastrophe filled him with horror.

Meanwhile, at the Tuileries, all were awaiting the return of the imperial party with the greatest anxiety.

What a triumphant return it was! Every house on the way was illuminated up to the very skylights. In the street, a dense crowd was swelling and surging about the carriage, and as it slowly advanced at a foot-pace, the prolonged roar of the multitude was heard like the sound of ocean waves coming from afar, and getting louder and louder as the carriage drew near—"Vive l'Empereur!"

All the attendants and ladies were grouped at the door to receive those who had borne the trial so bravely; but as the Empress crossed the threshold, for the first time her undaunted spirit failed her, and throwing herself into the arms of the Duchesse de Bassano, she burst into tears.

Some time after this terrible event, the chief

PRINCE JEROME.
FROM A PHOTOGRAPH BY LADREY-DISDERI.

PRINCESS MATHILDE.
FROM A PHOTOGRAPH BY LADREY-DISDERI.

secretary of the Empress (now deceased) came to my rooms one morning with a letter, which he asked me to interpret for him; it was in English, and although he thought he had gathered the sense, as the matter seemed important, he wished to be certain that he was not mistaken. It was addressed to the Empress; but according to the general rule in courts, all ordinary letters were opened and examined before being presented to her.

I saw immediately that the signature which had puzzled the secretary was that of the well-known Irish peer, the Marquis of Waterford. He wrote to warn the Empress that, to his certain knowledge, five hundred conspirators had sworn to risk their lives in turn, if necessary, to take that of the Emperor, unless he immediately gave some assurance of his intention of liberating Italy. Lord Waterford pleaded the cause of the Italians, and entreated the Empress to use her influence over the Emperor to induce him to take it in hand.

The communication was a serious one, and the secretary seemed much struck by it. Of course I told no one of what I had read, not even the family with whom I resided, and I never heard what impression had been produced on the Empress or the Emperor. But the Italian war began to loom in the future before long, and there were no more attempts on the Emperor's life. All the preceding conspiracies had been organized by Italians. Not one Frenchman ever tried to injure the Emperor, who was the people's friend, and who, till the fatal war with Germany, when the nation was maddened by its fearful reverses, was universally popular among the working classes. Even now, when complaints are made of hard times and penury, they always end with: "It was not so in the Emperor's time! Everything was prosperous then!"

His real adversaries belonged to a higher class of society.

As time went by, the duties of my situation at the palace, though still arduous, became gradually lighter, while the kindness shown to me from the beginning of my residence there ripened into intimacy and confidential friendship. My eldest pupil, being fully introduced into society, took up less and less of my time, as she shared more completely her mother's occupations and social duties, while the routine of my daily life was as agreeably diversified as possible. On innumerable occasions I shared the privileges of the household, including private views of various sights or exhibitions, reserved seats at the Emperor's reviews, the Emperor's boxes at the various operas or theaters, where I accompanied the ladies of the family once or twice every week, with all the advantages of the imperial carriage, and comfortable seats in boxes like small boudoirs. Occasionally, when some other engagement had prior claims, the entrance-ticket was handed over to me, and the private family carriage placed at my disposal, so that I could take friends with me and go independently.

The apartments of the palace were connected by long passages with doors of communication, so that it was possible to go all round the Tuileries and the Louvre without leaving the buildings, which led to much pleasant intercourse with our next neighbors on each side, the Archbishop of Bourges and the family of the Duc and Duchesse de Bassano, whose daughters were the intimate friends and constant companions of my youngest pupil, and of about the same age. The Archbishop held an ecclesiastical post of honor in the household, which called for his presence during a portion of the winter season. He was an intimate friend of the de Tascher family, and an almost daily visitor — a kind, genial old man, whom we all loved, of most venerable appearance, with his perfectly white hair and his gold episcopal cross resting on his purple cassock. He was passionately fond of the game of chess, and delighted in playing with me, or with one of my pupils to whom I had taught the game; but he was so unhappy when checkmated, that, according to the laughing suggestion of the old Count, I habitually allowed him to get the best of the game, only keeping up the battle sufficiently to give interest to the victory; but nothing could induce my pupil to do likewise. So the good Archbishop used to say, in perfect good faith, but rather ruefully: "I am really improving as a player; I can now beat 'Albion'; but I do not know how it is, I cannot manage little Hortense!"

The Count would then direct a mischievous glance toward me, and rub his hands with great glee.

Every winter fancy-costume balls, particularly liked by the Emperor and Empress, were given by the Duchesse de Tascher and Duchesse de Bassano, or by the ministers at their various official residences. I always went to these balls, usually accompanying the (Princess) Comtesse de Tascher, and wearing myself the convenient disguise of a domino. At the court official balls of the same kind, I was admitted (by an especial and very exceptional permission of the Empress) to the gallery surrounding the splendid "Salle des Maréchaux," where the imperial family were seated in state. I was generally alone there, or with my youngest pupil, and greatly enjoyed the magnificent sight.

From this gallery I saw the banquet, on the marriage of the Princess Clotilde, daughter of the King of Italy, with Prince Napoleon, and the fancy-costume ball which soon followed, where the young princess was dressed in a costume taken from a historical portrait in the Louvre gallery which was more artistic than suitable for her girlish figure and youthful appearance, with such a farthingale that her ladies were obliged to spread the crimson velvet robe over three chairs. The Emperor tried to dance with her, but it was noticed by the superstitious, as an unfavorable omen with regard to the Italian alliance, that he was repeatedly obliged to stop because the velvet folds wound around him in such a manner as to paralyze his movements, until at last he was obliged to give up the attempt in despair, and to take her back to her seat with a bow and a smile.

The Empress looked particularly beautiful that evening; she wore a Marie Antoinette head-dress of powdered hair, with a small round cap of scarlet satin adorned with emeralds and diamonds, surmounted by a heron's plume. Her costume was of a magnificent Lyons silk stuff of black and gold, opening at the sides over a scarlet satin underskirt; the bodice, cut square, was bordered with large emeralds and diamonds.

The Princess Clotilde was too much like her father to possess beauty, and was no rival for the Empress Eugénie; but her royal bearing and graceful figure were greatly admired. Unfortunately, the latter did not long retain the elegance of its lines.

CHAPTER VI

The Palais Royal—The imperial family—Unpleasant relations—Prince Jerome—Prince Napoleon—Princess Mathilde—Pierre Bonaparte—His sister Letitia—Prince Napoleon's speech in the Senate—Scene with the Emperor—Ball at the Hôtel d'Albe—The Empress and the page—Special invitation sent to me by the Empress—Princess Mathilde and Princess Clotilde—Contrast—The dresses of both—Intended costume of the Empress—Objections—The Empress and the paste-board horse—The Duc de Morny—His character—His marriage—Madame de Morny—"The White Mouse"—Scene with the Duc de Dino—Comte Walewski—His character and appearance—Comtesse Walewska.

THE Palais-Royal, where resided the younger branch of the reigning family, had at all times been a focus of opposition, and although the princes who resided there during the Empire owed everything to Napoleon III., the old traditions were, in this respect, thoroughly revived.

The poor Emperor, always kind, always gentle, always generous, was overpowered by the unpleasant relations coming to him from his great predecessor; so that he might well answer, as he did on one occasion, when reproached by the aged Prince Jerome,[1] with having "nothing" of his brother, the Emperor:

[1] The youngest brother of Napoleon I., father of the prince known by that name, and of the Princess Mathilde.

"I have his family!"

Not one of that uncomfortable family but caused him trouble in some way, while all clung to him with the cry of the leech: "Give! give!" And he gave—never refusing, even when he knew that he was favoring his enemies. Prince Jerome himself, and his son, Prince Napoleon. were never satisfied; then came Pierre Bonaparte,[1] whose low tastes and low habits were a constant source of annoyance; he was always in difficulties of some kind, requiring the Emperor's help. He married a woman of very inferior position and was never received at the court. His adventure with Victor Noir is well known; but here he seems to have really acted in self-defense. Unfortunately it was not the only instance of the kind.

Then came Letitia Bonaparte,[2] always in debt and always applying to the Emperor to pay her liabilities, with threats of coming out as an actress if he refused to do so. Her daughter married first a Hebrew banker named Solms; henceforward she entitled herself the "Princesse de Solms." Then she married the Italian demagogue Ratazzi, always engaged in conspiracies against the Emperor; finally, a Monsieur de Rute.

Prince Jerome, though far from cordial, or even grateful, was, however, too insignificant to be dangerous. I remember him only as a courteous old

---

[1] A son of Napoleon's brother Lucien.
[2] A daughter of Lucien.

man, very like his illustrious brother, with old-fashioned manners; holding ladies at arm's length by the tips of their fingers, and always most careful to address the Comtesse de Tascher as "Your Serene Highness." He had been king of Westphalia under the First Empire, and some people still spoke to him as "Sire" and "Your Majesty," but he was usually addressed as "Monseigneur" and "Your Imperial Highness."

His son, Prince Napoleon, was a more formidable opponent, although heartily disliked and despised by all classes and all political opinions outside a small circle of private friends. He possessed, however, brilliant talents, which, had he chosen to develop them, might have recalled something of the Napoleonic genius; whereas, in fact, he only caricatured the worst points of the Corsican adventurer, without showing any of the grand redeeming gifts of the great emperor.

The physical likeness was wonderful, but the expression was totally different. In the good portraits of Napoleon I., the clear eyes have a singularly piercing glance, at once conveying the idea of a commanding genius. With the same cast of features, there was something peculiarly low and thoroughly bad in the face of Prince Napoleon, which recalled in a striking manner the stamp of the worst Roman Caesars.

His will was despotic, his temper violent and brutal; his tastes were cynically gross, his language

PRINCE NAPOLEON AND PRINCESS CLOTILDE.
FROM A PHOTOGRAPH BY DISDÉRI & CO.

coarse beyond what could be imagined. While affecting tendencies of the most revolutionary and radical type, he was essentially a tyrant, and could brook no opposition to his will, always brutally expressed. He was jealous of the Emperor's preëminent position, as of something stolen from himself; but, though in a state of chronic rebellion, he never hesitated to accept all the worldly advantages which the title of "cousin" could obtain for him.

The Emperor felt a sort of indulgent affection for Prince Napoleon, and had the latter chosen to make use of his undeniable talents, in accordance with the duties of the position which he had accepted, he might, during the Empire, have played an important political part, and have gathered the Emperor's inheritance at the death of the Prince Imperial.

But never were natural gifts so misapplied or so wasted. He could bear no restraint, no interruption in his life of sensual pleasures, and he never persevered in anything that he undertook, when any personal sacrifice was required to carry it out. Everything that he attempted bore the stamp of sudden impulse never followed up. He seemed to delight in outraging public opinion, and so constantly played the proverbial part of the "bull in the china shop" that the Emperor was kept in a state of constant anxiety as to what "Napoléon" would choose to do next.

His refusal to drink the health of the Empress,

in her presence, on her birthday,[1] is one of the many instances of his utter disregard of the manners and habits of a gentleman, while his real feeling toward the Emperor was betrayed on more than one occasion.

After the Pianori attempt on the Emperor's life, when Prince Napoleon came to present his official congratulations, his face was so eloquent of what lay below that the Empress, turning to one of her ladies, whispered in English: "Look at the Prince Napoleon!"

After his famous revolutionary speech in the Senate, which brought down upon him the withering response of the Duc d'Aumale ("Letter on the History of France"), the Emperor sent for him, roused to such a pitch of indignation that his voice, usually so peculiarly soft and low, was heard raised in anger even in the distant waiting-room of the attendants; for he well knew what the effect would be on the Conservative Imperialists.

There was a violent scene, and when Prince Napoleon returned to the Palais Royal, he vented his fury on a magnificent vase of Sèvres porcelain, which he dashed to pieces. And yet I remember that the Duc de Tascher, who had said to me that he "would rather serve the King of Dahomey than such a man," still acknowledged, with unwilling admiration: "But

---

[1] The Emperor had desired him to propose the health of the Empress; he persistently begged to be excused, notwithstanding the indignant expostulations of the Emperor.— See Mérimée's "Letters to Panizzi."

what an orator! He looked as handsome as Lucifer himself."

The opinion of his own personal friends, as to what his future rule was likely to be, may be gathered from the answer of one belonging to his most intimate circle, to whom (after the fall of the Empire) Prince Napoleon said, "If ever I am emperor, you shall have an important post."

"Monseigneur," was the comment, in the laughing tone needful for the acceptance of a bold remark, "if ever you should be at the head of public affairs, I would take to my heels the very next day, for you would not be easy to deal with."

He was not offended at the blunt frankness of the speaker, for he was acute enough to despise sycophants, and to appreciate independence even in those who made him understand that they would not endure his unmannerly ways. On such occasions, he has been known to say, by way of apology: "Oh, my dear ——, excuse me, *I am ill-bred*" ("Je suis mal-élevé").

With his democratic opinions and plebeian tastes, he was, in strange contrast, extremely proud—the pride of birth, inherited from his German mother, the Princess Catherine of Würtemberg. He had royal blood in his veins, and was as determined to carry out *ebenbürtig* (equal birth) requirements as any prince of the German Confederacy.

He looked down loftily on the Emperor as the

son of a private gentlewoman,[1] and the husband of another, chosen voluntarily. "I am of too great lineage for that" was a saying of his; and his ambition was finally gratified by obtaining the hand of a king's daughter, the descendant of an ancient royal line.

Prince Napoleon's sister, the Princess Mathilde, was not likely to be a congenial friend to the young and innocent bride. With the same striking Bonaparte cast of features as her brother, she was, like him, "ill-bred"; in fact, the Corsican semi-barbarian, such as the great Emperor himself, has been revealed to us by contemporary memoirs. She had possessed great beauty, and in her youth was betrothed to Prince Louis Napoleon, afterward Napoleon III.

She hated the Empress Eugénie, of whom she spoke in offensive terms. As years went by, though still retaining the classical lines of her characteristic features, she had become as coarse in her personal appearance as in her language and manners. She was clever and artistically gifted, and was principally surrounded by men belonging to literary and artistic sets. She was very good-natured to all around her, and a kind, sympathizing friend in need.

I had an opportunity of particularly remarking the strange contrast between the two sisters-in-law, at a ball which was an event in the fashionable

---

[1] Hortense de Beauharnais, daughter of Josephine by her first husband, and married to Louis Bonaparte, King of Holland.

world, about a year after the marriage of Prince Napoleon.

The Empress had built a very beautiful residence for the use of her sister, the Duchess of Alva, on her visits to Paris. This villa, or *hôtel*, as it is called in French, with its garden, had been decorated and adorned with unsparing expense, under the superintendence of the Duc de Tascher, whose artistic taste gave a character to the whole far superior to the mere upholstery prettiness which the Empress favored in her usual arrangements.

When all was ready, the Empress, by way of inauguration, chose to give a fancy ball outside of the court, "as a private individual," where only those whom she was pleased to have would be invited. She made out the lists herself, but notwithstanding all her restrictions the unavoidable number admitted was so considerable that it became necessary to build out into the garden a temporary room for the supper-tables. This beautiful banqueting hall was arranged by the Duc de Tascher in imitation of the great picture by Paul Veronese, "The Marriage of Cana" (in the Louvre Gallery), with most effective results. A curtain concealed the entrance till it was drawn at a given signal, when the orchestra played the march from Meyerbeer's "Prophète," while the guests descended the steps of a magnificent staircase on which medieval pages, dressed in the Guzman-Montijo colors, stood, holding gilt candelabra, and motionless as statues.

An amusing incident occurred while the pages were rehearsing the part they had to play in these festivities. They were chosen among the diminutive grooms of the Emperor's stables, and when the costume was ready, a pretty boy, who seemed about twelve years of age, was brought to the Empress for her examination and approval. The dress pleased her, and she turned the boy round to inspect him fully, setting his velvet cap jauntily on his curls, which she arranged to her satisfaction, adjusting his ruff, etc. Then kindly patting his cheek, she inquired:

"How old are you, my little friend?"

"*Twenty*, Madame!"

The scream of dismay which followed, and the amusement of the bystanders, may be imagined.

With her usual kindness, and happily, in this instance, with less compromising results, the Empress sent me by the Duc de Tascher, but from her own hand, a card of invitation to this ball, with a message that it would be worth seeing, and that she particularly wished me to be present. The (Princesse) Comtesse de Tascher immediately said that I should go with her, and that she would be glad to have my arm, while, of course, I was equally glad to have her protection and chaperonage.

Accordingly, when the great day came, we went together, early, in the imperial carriage, for which every one made way, and, wearing masks and dominoes, we took our seats near the entrance, where the Duc and Duchesse de Tascher, representing the Empress, received the guests, so as to watch all the arrivals. After some time, we heard peals of laughter coming from the opposite end of the gallery where we were seated, and turning to look, we saw a woman of bold appearance and manners, surrounded by men.

"That woman must have had a card given her by some one," remarked the Comtesse de Tascher; adding, "I hope she will be turned out—her style is dreadful."

Presently the noisy group came toward us, and the Countess started.

"Oh, my dear! Look!" she exclaimed, "It is the Princess Mathilde!"

She came close to us; and there she was, undoubtedly—but not immediately recognizable, because her skin was dyed brown. She wore the costume of an Egyptian "fellah" woman—very artistic, certainly, but more suitable for an artist's model than for a civilized member of society.

As she stood—with her circle of men around her, talking and laughing noisily—while the dominoes, ever privileged for impertinence, pursued her unfortunate lady-in-waiting, pertinaciously inquiring: "Did *you* paint your princess?"—the Comtesse de Tascher touched my arm. I turned, and there, opposite to her sister-in-law, near an open doorway, stood the Princess Clotilde, with an expression of dismayed amazement on her grave young face. She was very simply dressed in pink and white silk as a conventional shepherdess; the only remarkable detail of her costume being a wreath of pink roses, separated by large diamonds, worn as a necklace close round her throat. No contrast could be more striking than was then presented between the gipsy woman and the fair young creature, all innocence and purity in her simple girlish attire, yet so unmistakably royal in her bearing. She stood motionless and silent as if petrified, without seeking recognition from the strange group before her, and, after a pause, turned and walked away gravely. But the Princess Clotilde never again went to a fancy ball, and quietly expressed her determination, which was irrevocable. "No; I will go to ordinary balls, but not to costume balls." "But why, Madame?" "I will not go." This was all, and she vouchsafed no explanation. But what I had seen gave me the key to a resolution which caused general surprise.

The Empress had intended to appear as a conventional Louis Quinze Diana, with powdered hair and a profusion of diamonds, but there had been much discussion as to whether or not she ought to wear this dress. There was no impropriety in the arrangement of the costume itself, which I saw, on another occasion, worn by the young and very pretty Princess Anna Murat,[1] to whom the Empress had

---

[1] A descendant of the Marshal, who was for some time king of Naples, and of his wife, Caroline Bonaparte, one of the first Emperor's sisters.

DUC DE MORNY.
FROM A PHOTOGRAPH BY BRAUN CLÉMENT & CO.

DUCHESSE DE MORNY.
FROM A PHOTOGRAPH BY LADREY-DISDÉRI.

given it, after being reluctantly persuaded that it was unsuitable to the dignity of her position. It was not easy to make the Empress understand that she could not do what other people did, and that many things must be abstained from — though unobjectionable in others. On this occasion the dress was prepared and laid out in the room reserved for her use, and while still undecided as to whether or not she would appear as Diana, she examined what was in readiness for a fancy quadrille, in which some of the dancers were to figure with the pasteboard horses seen in a circus, where the apparent rider moves inside the trappings. This took her fancy, and she immediately made the trial of one herself; but once inside she could not get out again, and none of her ladies knew how to extricate her.

Finally, Comte Robert de Tascher was called to the rescue, and succeeded in removing the inconvenient appendage, while the Empress was much amused by the adventure. He came to tell us of it in the ballroom, adding the information that she had decided not to wear the Diana dress, and that she would be present concealed in a domino.

Among the most remarkable of the distinguished guests at this ball was the Duc de Morny, who was known to be a son of the Emperor's mother, Queen Hortense, a very questionable honor, which, however, he put forward on every possible occasion, in a manner showing a complete absence of all innate delicacy of feeling. In appearance his gentlemanlike demeanor and perfect courtly grace were unsurpassed; but, nevertheless, the flower of the hydrangea, called by the French *Hortensia*, surmounted by a royal crown, figured significantly on the panels of his carriage, and in general nothing that could recall his birth was left aside.

After his special embassy to Russia, on the occasion of the coronation of Alexander II., he married a young Princess Troubetskoï, to whom an origin of the same kind as his own (attributed to the Emperor Nicholas) was ascribed by public rumor. On which Morny said cynically: "I am the son of a queen—the brother of an emperor—the son-in-law of an emperor—*et c'est tout naturel.*"

Even at the court of Napoleon III., where there was not much austerity of principle, the effrontery of this speech caused disgust.

Morny was very like the Emperor, but much better-looking; of taller and finer figure, with more elegance and charm of manner. He was guided only by self-interest, and was esteemed by none; but his natural cleverness, his determined spirit, and the wonderful power of attracting the most unwilling, made him a valuable auxiliary to the Emperor, to whom his loss was an irreparable misfortune.

His wife was one of those strange beings, of whom there were several instances in the society of that day, whose tempers, whims, and caprices would have required energetic repression in the case of children of six years old, but were absolutely astonishing to meet with among women supposed to have reached years of discretion. Madame de Morny was very pretty; but her fragile little figure was as thin as a skeleton, with small hands like a bird's claws. Her features were very delicate, and her pale complexion of dazzling fairness; but her tiny nose was as sharp as a needle, and her dark eyes had a fierce, waspish expression, the very reverse of attractive. The sharp black eyes were in startling contrast to her flaxen hair, which was so light as to be almost silvery, so that she was called "La Souris Blanche" (the White Mouse).

At the ball I have been describing, she figured in a fancy dance of sixteen ladies, representing the four Elements, and, of course, was one of those personifying "Air," dressed with floating streamers of gauzy blue and white. When the dance was over, it was followed by another, representing the characters of the fairy tales of our childhood; and Madame de Morny sat down by the Comtesse de Tascher and myself to see the dance. But the Duc de Dino, who had chosen the extraordinary disguise of the "stump of a tree," swathed in bands of brown linen, like a mummy, with all the supposed young shoots standing out like a bush round his head, brought his unwelcome figure just before us. Being a small man, he was exactly on our level, the bush forming a complete screen. We were all annoyed, though naturally silent; but Madame de Morny, addressing him in a haughty, imperious tone, cried: "Ôtez-vous de là!" ("Go away from here!"). He turned, looked at her from head to foot with ineffable disdain, and did not move. She uttered a fierce growl, and, like a small tigress, flew at him, seizing him by the branches round his head, and trying to pull him forcibly aside. He took no notice, and failing in her attempt, she was forced to sit down, in a state of fury.

Such an exhibition of temper in a court ball-room may give some idea of the home delights which she provided for her husband. I remember a large official dinner-party, where the de Tascher family were among the guests, and where the Duc de Morny was obliged to do the honors alone, because in a fit of temper and caprice his wife refused to appear. He was, however, quite equal to the occasion, and to others of the same kind, playing his part of host with his usual charming grace and apparently unruffled equanimity.

A great contrast to Morny was found in Comte Walewski, another of the celebrated men who figured at the court and councils of Napoleon III. Here, too, was a "bend sinister," sufficiently revealed by his striking likeness to Napoleon I., but a more agreeable version of the well-known face than that of Prince Napoleon. General Comte de Tascher had, among many others, a small portrait of the great Emperor which, he told me, was the best likeness he had seen. This portrait seemed reproduced in Comte Walewski; the features, the peculiar pallor, the shade of the gray-blue eyes and their expression, were strikingly similar. But, unlike Morny, he had the good taste to keep the explanation in the background. At a court reception he happened to hear a lady say to another: "How wonderfully like *his father!*" He turned, and with that stiff, rather haughty demeanor which made him in some degree unpopular, he gravely remarked: "I was not aware, madame, that *Comte Walewski* had the honor of being personally known to you!"

He was not considered agreeable, showing too much of the "statesman" even in private life; but he was a gentleman, and more esteemed than Morny, although not so much liked. His wife, however, greatly assisted him in retaining some popularity by her particularly graceful and amiable manners. Every one was attracted by the Comtesse Walewska, who never lost an opportunity of doing a kind act, or of obliging others in those small things of daily life which are so pleasing and so valuable. She was also quiet and ladylike. Her beauty was much extolled, but this seemed more due to a general impression of a very charming and most agreeable woman, than to real beauty taken in a literal sense.

CHAPTER VII

Princess Clotilde — Her religious fervor — Her daily life — Her court — Evenings at the Palais-Royal — Ennui of the Empress Eugénie — The camp at Châlons — Enmity of the aristocratic Faubourg St. Germain — Persistent criticisms; irritation of the Empress — The Comte de Chambord and the Comtesse de Tascher — The great official balls at the Tuileries — The "Cent-gardes" — The soldier with sugar-plums in his boot — The Empress and the sentinel — A wager — Etiquette of the balls — The balcony of the "Salle des Maréchaux" — Clever answer of Mademoiselle de Montijo — Costume balls — The police — The fancy quadrilles — Taglioni.

THE Princess Clotilde, whom every one watched with pitying interest, had now settled down into her regular life; and it soon became evident to all that it would have been impossible to choose anywhere a wife more utterly uncongenial to Prince Napoleon. She was, and is still, a princess of medieval times, a Saint Elizabeth of Hungary, neither very highly educated nor very clever, caring only for her religious practices and her works of charity. She soon ceased to pay much attention to her toilet, reaching even the point of carelessness, which greatly annoyed her husband. It must be acknowledged that the devotion of the Princess Clotilde went perhaps beyond what was quite judicious; but no one had any influence over her, and what she considered her duty was performed with a sort of gentle, placid stubbornness which allowed of no expostulation.

At first she showed particular graciousness to my elder pupil, the future Princess Thurn und Taxis, who was about her own age, and whose manners evidently pleased her. Had this first sympathetic intercourse been encouraged they might have reached friendly intimacy, but the de Tascher de la Pageries, being on the Beauharnais side of the imperial family, were never on very cordial terms with the Bonapartes, and the Princes Napoleon and Jerome were particularly disliked by the Duc de Tascher; consequently the intercourse with the Palais Royal was limited to strict courtly etiquette and politeness.

The ladies who had been first appointed to attend the Princess Clotilde were treated with such rudeness by Prince Napoleon, that one after another sent in her resignation; so that, finally, the Princess had only around her ladies chosen out of the circle composed of his friends and their wives, whose ways and opinions were in opposition to all her own. The style and language of her sister-in-law, the Princess Mathilde, could only shock her feelings, and she was not attracted by the gay doings of the imperial court, where she only appeared on necessary occasions, being herself accustomed to traditional etiquette, and combining the pride of rank, which she considered proper dignity, with her very real Christian humility. "She is a true princess!" was commonly said of her. At the present time she attends the poor like a hospital sister, wearing hospital aprons, and shrinking from no act of charity, however repulsive; but although, when she rises, she dresses without assistance, her attendants are required to be within reach and in readiness to give their services, because it is proper that such should be the case; no usage of etiquette is overlooked, because it is right that she should be treated as a royal princess.

During the Empire, even in her early youth, no one dared to show the least familiarity in her presence; but the stiff decorum of her circle did not make home life particularly agreeable. During the day, her ladies accompanied her to the churches, where they unwillingly awaited her pleasure for hours; in the evening they were seated round a table with their work, while the Princess herself diligently plied her needle, speaking very little and not encouraging any one else to do so. Some ladies, accustomed more to the brusque ways of the master of the house than to the tact required in the presence of a king's daughter, tried to speak of public affairs, wondering, for instance, how matters would end between Victor Emmanuel and Pope Pius IX., which must evidently have been most displeasing to the Princess Clotilde. Scarcely looking up, she replied very gently, but so as to effectually silence the indiscreet talkers: "The intentions

PRINCE NAPOLEON.
FROM A PHOTOGRAPH BY LADREY-DISDERI.

COMTE DE WALEWSKI.
FROM A PHOTOGRAPH BY LADREY-DISDERI.

are good—matters are in God's hands, and what is his will must happen." But never to any one did she express her private opinions, or utter anything more definite than such truisms. She lived alone, and had no confidential friends. That such a home should have been unutterably wearisome to Prince Napoleon is not surprising; though it is doubtful whether any wife, however gifted, could have retained any hold upon his affections.

The Empress Eugénie had hoped to find a congenial friend in the young and interesting bride, but she soon discovered that intimacy would be impossible. The Princess was cold, dignified, and not devoid of a perceptible shade of haughtiness; withal, intensely devout; while the Empress, notwithstanding all that has been said of her "clerical" tendencies, was at that time only very moderately religious, a victim to "ennui," and ready for anything that could diversify the monotony of her life.

One of the chamberlains told me that, as he preceded the Emperor and Empress on one occasion, he heard the Emperor remonstrating on her love of pleasure, and the fatigue which it often caused her. She answered that she could not help it,—that she was dying of "ennui,"—winding up by an earnest entreaty to be taken with him to the camp at Châlons. The Emperor strongly objected —a camp of soldiery would be no place for her— she would be very uncomfortable—besides, what possible attraction could she find there?

As usual, the Empress had her own way; she went to the camp, and slept in a tent, with an umbrella over her bed, because the rain came through; she walked about among the troops, with mud up to her ankles, protected by gaiters—and was delighted. Anything for a change.

But such a proceeding had no precedent in former reigns, and was much criticized. The lofty enmity of the Faubourg St. Germain, who looked down contemptuously upon everything said or done by "Mademoiselle de Montijo,"—for they did not even vouchsafe to call her "Madame Bonaparte,"—especially stung her to the quick, and after shrinking at first from their criticism, she became irritated, even to recklessness. "Those people all seem to despise me, and to look down upon me as an inferior," she said bitterly, "and yet, surely, the blue blood of Spain is worth something!"

"High life below stairs?" was the remark made to me, in English, by a leader of fashion in the dreaded Faubourg, where I had retained friends and family connections, many of whom would not, at first, visit me in my new abode at the Tuileries.

"Why do you keep bad company?" was their answer when I remonstrated.

I remember the stately dignity with which the (Princesse) Comtesse de Tascher said, when an invitation was refused by a Legitimist on the plea that his political opinions did not allow him to accept it:

"He is more particular than his master, for when

the Comte de Chambord came to Munich, he immediately paid me a visit, coming himself to my house!"

In the winter there were always four State balls, attended by a motley crowd, since, for the sake of popularity, invitations were as much extended as possible, and generally reached the number of from four to five thousand. Still, these crowded balls, though much disliked by the court and accepted as a necessary evil, were a splendid sight not easily to be forgotten.

The entrance was under the "Pavillon de l'Horloge," in the center of the building, where a large staircase adorned with a profusion of plants and flowers led to the "Galerie de la Paix," where the guests remained till the Emperor and Empress had taken their seats in the "Salle des Maréchaux." On each step of the staircase stood two of the "Centgardes" (the Emperor's body-guard) in their brilliant uniform of pale blue turned up with crimson, their bright steel cuirass and helmet. They were all picked men, sub-officers chosen out of various regiments, of magnificent appearance, who, when on duty, stood motionless as statues. This absolute immobility is said to be so fatiguing that it cannot be sustained beyond a limited time; but it was so complete that to come suddenly on one of these guards in the palace was positively startling; it was scarcely possible to believe that they were alive.

One day the little Prince, in childish play, emptied a whole bag of sugar-plums into the boot of the sentinel before his door, hoping to provoke some sign of life, but without the slightest effect on the military statue before him.

In the evening the incident was mentioned by the Empress in the presence of Colonel Verly, who commanded the regiment. He then declared the drill to be so perfect that "nothing" would make one of his men move when on duty. The Empress would not believe this assertion, and finally laid a wager that she would make one of the guards move. The wager was accepted by Colonel Verly, and the Empress then went with him into the neighboring gallery, where they walked backward and forward before the sentinel, the Empress trying by every means to attract his attention. The man stood as if turned into stone. Colonel Verly smiled. The Empress then, with her characteristic impetuosity, went straight up to the guard, and (according to familiar speech) "boxed his ears." Not a muscle moved. The Empress then acknowledged that Colonel Verly had won the day, and sent a handsome compensation to the soldier, who proudly refused it, saying that he was sufficiently compensated by the honor of having had his sovereign lady's hand on his cheek.

In the terrible war of 1870 with Germany these fine troops proved that they were not intended merely for parade, but took their place gloriously among the bravest.

The Emperor and Empress on leaving their private apartments first entered the "Salon du Premier Consul," where they received the Imperial family, the guests admitted to formal presentation, the ambassadors, and other important dignitaries. Then, followed by the brilliant assembly, they entered the "Salle des Maréchaux" in state, where, in a loud voice, "L'Empereur!" was announced. The imperial party then took their seats on a slightly raised platform, and the dancing began, both in the "Galerie de la Paix" and the "Salle des Maréchaux," with a double orchestra.

The latter room, which was the finest in the palace, derived its name from the portraits of the great Napoleon's marshals, which figured on the walls—twelve in number—like the peers of Charlemagne!

On each side, but of course closed at night, was a large balcony; one, looking on the gardens, where all the queens and princesses of France had stood to be presented to the people after their marriage, and where the Empress had also appeared as the Emperor's bride on returning from Notre Dame. The other balcony opened on the "Place du Carrousel," and there the Empress sat, with her "service d'honneur," when the Emperor reviewed the troops, followed as soon as possible, and perhaps sooner than was prudent, by the little Prince in uniform, riding his pony with such spirit, even when a young child, that a burst of enthusiasm from the troops always greeted his appearance.

It was said that when the Emperor was still President of the French Republic, shortly before the proclamation of the Empire, he complimented Mademoiselle de Montijo and her mother with seats on this privileged balcony, to witness a review. As he passed before her, on horseback, he looked up, saying:

"How can I reach you, Mademoiselle?"

"By way of *the chapel*, Monseigneur," was the quick and acute reply; for the entrance, leading to the chapel on one side, was, on the other, the most direct way to reach the "Salle des Maréchaux" from the place where he was speaking.

There was always one costume ball every year, but, of course, much more restricted in the number of the guests than the great balls before mentioned. The Empress always appeared in costume, seated in state, surrounded by the imperial family, also in costume; but the Emperor never went beyond a change of uniform. The great interest of the time was the question of the fancy quadrilles which were always danced before the platform on which their Majesties were seated. These quadrilles, which varied every year, were usually got up by the ladies de Tascher, who thoroughly understood such matters, and were carefully rehearsed for some time previously, under the direction of Mérante, the ballet-master of the opera, who composed dances suitable for ladies not wearing ballet costumes. For instance, one year a gipsy party appeared, dancing a Hungarian dance to the music of Weber's "Preciosa"; the next, a whole scene of the time of Louis XVI. was given—the Duchesse de Tascher, in a gilded and painted sedan-chair, carried by her servants in livery, surrounded by pages and ladies of the period, and escorted by courtiers of the time, the whole ending in a minuet, as danced at the court of Louis XVI.; another year it was a quadrille in Polish dresses, the dancers drawn in sledges, and then dancing a spirited mazurka, etc., etc. At one of the rehearsals of these dances, I was told that the celebrated Taglioni was present: my curiosity was greatly awakened, having heard my father and mother speak of her airy grace with absolute enthusiasm, and I eagerly asked the Comtesse de G—— to point her out to me.

"Hush!" she replied, "she is just behind you."

I took an opportunity of turning round, and there I saw a remarkably stiff-looking person, with pursed-up mouth and very prim appearance, absolutely the conventional type of a pedantic school-mistress. I never was more astonished. Mérante had wished to have her opinion of the dance; but she spoke very little, and seemed the reverse of agreeable or natural.

The costume balls at the residences of the different ministers, or in the apartments of the Duchesse de Tascher or the Duchesse de Bassano, were more agreeable for the Emperor and Empress than the official balls, for they came in masks and dominos, enjoying complete liberty. The Emperor, however, was easily recognized by his peculiar walk and attitude; I once came near him unexpectedly in a doorway (where he stood with other dominos, who evidently accompanied him) and knew him at once, involuntarily drawing back. He seemed annoyed, and made a gesture as if to say: "What are you stopping for?" when, of course, I passed on without taking any further notice.

When a ball took place in the private apartments of the dignitaries of the household, and it was known that the Emperor and Empress would be present, great precautions were taken for their safety, especially in the case of costume balls, where masks were tolerated and of course constituted a serious danger. All guests wearing masks were required to remove them before entering the ballrooms to allow their features to be examined; detectives stood about the entrance and mingled with the guests; many of them were dressed as attendants, and carried trays of refreshments through the rooms.

CHAPTER VIII

The police force during the Empire — Story of M. de Saint-Julien — A robbery — A fascinating detective — A mysterious sign — Dinner parties at the palace — The imperial table during Lent and on Fridays — Lent concerts — Auber — Mario — Patti — Alboni — The national tune composed by Queen Hortense — The Emperor's dislike of music — The mechanical piano — The "Stabat Mater" performed in the chapel — The supposed excessive devotion of the Empress.

THE police force of the Empire was a curious and complicated institution, but it cannot be denied that in those days life and property enjoyed a degree of security which afterward did not exist. A remarkable instance of the acuteness shown was related to me by a personage concerned in it, the Comte de G—— F——, well known in the highest Parisian society of that time.

The Comte de G—— F—— was intimate with an old Marchioness of the aristocratic Faubourg St. Germain; he had known her for many years, and even had the habit of addressing her by the affectionate term of "Maman."

One day on paying "Maman" a visit, he found her in a state of great agitation; she had just discovered that she had been robbed of a large sum of money, which she had placed in her bureau pending its investment by her *agent de change*, or stock-broker.

The Count soothed her as well as he could, and having ascertained that she had not yet mentioned what she had just discovered to any one but himself, he urged her to keep the matter secret, and to leave the management of it in his hands, which she consented to do.

The Count then went at once to the chief of the police, who listened attentively, and, merely remarking that the theft must have been committed by some one well acquainted with the house, asked carelessly what were the habits of the Marchioness. The Count answered that she led the quiet life of an elderly lady, only varied by a dinner-party every week, on that very day; but that she was so much disturbed by her loss that probably on this occasion the guests would be put off.

"On no account!" cried the prefect of police. "Tell your friend above all things to make no change; she must give her dinner-party as usual—but she must allow me to send her a guest."

The Count started. "What—a detective? My friend will not like the idea at all."

"If she wishes to recover her money, she must let me manage this matter in my own way. Be so kind as to go to the Passage Delorme, opposite the Tuileries Palace, at five o'clock this evening. You will there find a young man who will address you by name, and who will call himself 'M. de Saint-Julien.' You will take him to your friend, and he will join her party. Leave the rest to me."

A good deal disturbed, the Count returned to the Marchioness, who at first was horrified at the idea of a detective for a guest; but she yielded at length, and the Count went, as agreed, to the Passage Delorme. The gallery was empty, and the Count began to look into the shop windows to beguile the time, when he saw a young man fashionably dressed, and of remarkably elegant and gentlemanlike appearance, who also began to look at the toys. After a short pause he accosted the Count.

"Monsieur, you are, I believe, waiting for some one?"

"Monsieur," answered the Count, "I am, indeed, expecting some one to meet me; but I should be greatly surprised if that individual were yourself."

"I have the pleasure of addressing the Comte de G—— F——?"

"Yes."

"I am M. de Saint-Julien."

Greatly astonished, the Count bowed, and at once began to pace the gallery with the new-comer, who questioned him with astute quickness as to the circumstances of the robbery, and, after quietly stating his opinion that the thief must be some one well acquainted with the ways of the Marchioness, he added:

"Now take me to your friend's house."

"But," said the Count, "how shall I know if you have discovered any clue?"

"I will make this gesture," and the detective made a rapid circular motion with his right hand, holding the forefinger extended.

This point being settled, "M. de Saint-Julien" was duly introduced to the Marchioness. Soon he had charmed every one present by his perfect ease of manner and the brilliancy of his conversation.

The Count sat gravely watching the strange guest, little pleased at his apparent forgetfulness of the only motive which explained his presence in such society. But at the close of the dinner M. de Saint-Julien, still carelessly talking and laughing, looked toward the Count, and rapidly passed his hand, with forefinger extended, round the brim of the finger-glass before him, but in such a manner that it seemed the natural accompaniment to what he was saying.

On leaving the dinner-table, the Count eagerly approached him, and whispered:

"You made the sign?"

"Certainly."

"You are on the track?"

"I know who it is."

"Who?" cried the Count.

"The servant who was behind your chair. He is the man."

"How can you possibly know?" exclaimed the Count, greatly astonished.

"I suspected that the robbery had been committed by a professional thief, so I used words and expressions which, although they would not attract your notice, yet, as I employed them, had another meaning in the thieves' dialect or *argot*. The man at once recognized in me a police officer, and turned pale. He is the thief."

"But," cried the Count, "of course he will now try to escape!"

"Do you take me for a fool?" said M. de Saint-Julien. "The house is guarded at every door."

The man really did try to escape, and was immediately stopped. The room in which he slept was then searched, and the whole sum was found except a few francs, spent probably at some *café*.

A few months later the Count was walking on the Terrasse des Feuillants, in the gardens of the Tuileries, when he met a policeman in the usual dress of his class, with a good-humored but very ordinary expression of countenance, wearing the small mustache and pointed beard of the *sergent de ville*. The man accosted him, and was not recognized till he revealed himself as "M. de Saint-Julien."

Every Thursday there was a large dinner party at the palace, followed by a "reception," where the Empress took the greatest pains to propitiate every one present, going from one to another, remembering what to say to each of her guests, and allowing no one to feel neglected.

The Emperor's table was said by the Duc de Tascher to be the best royal table in Europe. Dinner was served very rapidly, and never lasted more than an hour. For the sake of avoiding all risk to the ladies' dresses, the dishes were offered in a low voice to each guest, but they did not help themselves. The plate was handed with its contents ready. This vexed the Duc de Tascher, who often protested to the servants, saying that they always gave him what he did not want, much to the amusement of his neighbors at the imperial table.

On Fridays, and the fast-days of the Church, two dinners were served: one according to ecclesiastical prescription, the other as usual. Those present chose according to their wishes.

In Lent several concerts took place at the palace—it might be supposed as a penance, for the Emperor and Empress both particularly disliked music. Of course at these concerts the most celebrated artists appeared; but the Emperor never went beyond quiet resignation, even when listening to Mario and Patti. No music was welcome to him, but he particularly hated the tune which was a sort of national air during the Empire—"Partant pour la Syrie," composed by his mother, Queen Hortense, and which followed him pertinaciously wherever he went. He would then say with a sigh: "Ah! my poor mother did not foresee what she would inflict on me, when she composed that tune!"

Strange to say, with such an unmusical father and

mother, the Prince Imperial was passionately fond of music, which rather alarmed the Emperor, who, with amusing anxiety, expressed the earnest hope that he would not compose operas some day.

The Duc de Tascher was a good judge of music, and had a particular horror of the mechanical piano used for dancing. When it was first introduced, he heard one morning the voluble notes as though some one were skimming over the keys of a piano, and expressed his indignation to the Emperor.

"There was a fellow playing this morning—I cannot imagine who it can be—who has nimble fingers enough, but who plays like a perfect ass, without the least soul or musical feeling."

The Emperor answered quietly: "I am that individual—I played this morning."

"Good heavens, Sire, how could I suppose such a thing! I never in my life heard of your playing any instrument, or caring for music!"

The Emperor, after enjoying his discomfiture for a few moments, explained that the piano was mechanical and that he had simply turned the handle!

As we did not share the imperial aversion to music, the concerts in Lent were a great delight to my pupils and myself, as we always obtained leave from the Duc de Bassano to attend at the rehearsals in the "Salle des Maréchaux." Auber, the composer, was always present, superintending the artists and the Conservatoire, who took the choruses. He was a small, meager old man, with gray hair and an aquiline nose, but still very active and keenly interested when his own music was performed, though taking matters coolly when other composers suffered from imperfect interpretation. He well knew the real feeling of the imperial hosts, for, once especially, I saw him spring to his feet during the interminable duet in the first act of "Guillaume Tell," and stop the performers.

"You must cut that down; they will never endure it!" he said, thus boldly interpreting what had been my own private feeling for some time.

Adelina Patti appeared at these concerts in the very beginning of her musical career; looking like a mere girl, almost a child. She sang with Mario, as a duet, the drinking song in "La Traviata," "Libiamo," with beautiful effect, each singer feeling the value of the other, and both doing their best. But all the great singers, both French and Italian, were heard in turn at these concerts, which we greatly enjoyed as may be supposed, though the lofty room was very cold on such occasions, and the singers complained. I remember Madame Gueymard, the prima donna of the French opera, insisting upon having a warm footstool during the rehearsal, and standing upon it when called to express her affliction in "Ah! che la morte" of "Il Trovatore," which she sang with her husband, who stood at some distance to give due effect to his lamentations, answered by her sobs. "Addio, Leonora!" "My dear, *what* are you about? — you are all wrong." "Addio, Leonora!" etc., etc.

NAPOLEON III., THE EMPRESS EUGÉNIE,
AND THE PRINCE IMPERIAL.

FROM A PHOTOGRAPH BY LAFREY-DISDERI.

These insights into green-room mysteries were extremely amusing to us; but sometimes the very great singers, too sure of their powers, such as Alboni, disappointed us by merely humming a tune to try it with the orchestra, instead of singing it. Happily this was a rare occurrence, as they mostly exercised their voices to judge of the effect in the room.

On Thursday of Holy Week, Rossini's "Stabat Mater" was sung in the chapel by the first artists; all the ladies present were dressed in black, with black lace veils, the effect of which was very solemn.

A great deal has been said as to the ultra devotion of the Empress. That her sorrows and reverses have awakened fervent religious feelings is no doubt true; but at that time there was certainly no tendency to excess. She never went to any church but the chapel of the Tuileries, where the services were limited to the daily masses, which she did not habitually attend, and the Sunday high mass. There were no afternoon services of any kind, and no sermons, excepting in Lent, or on very particular occasions. At Christmas, the midnight mass, so much appreciated by Catholics, was always celebrated, but the court never attended officially. The de Tascher family and some other ladies were always present, but I never saw the Empress appear even in the gallery.

CHAPTER IX

"The Empress's Mondays" — Orders worn by ladies — The court train — The "Salut du Trône," or grand court obeisance — The inclosed garden at the Tuileries — "Bagatelle" — The court leaves Paris — Fontainebleau — "La Régie" — Inconvenience of living in a palace — Housewifely care of the Empress — A siege in the apartments — A prince left at the door — St. Cloud — Villeneuve l'Étang — Furniture embroidered by Josephine — A collation with the Prince Imperial — Anecdotes — A "Te Deum" wanted.

AFTER Easter the great official festivities were replaced by the more valued and more select balls called "the Empress's Mondays," at which her gracious kindness could more easily be appreciated. For these the most elegant toilets were reserved. The guests were received in the private apartments, and each one could attract more notice than in the "crush" of the state balls, where the very rich toilets were almost wasted.

Some ladies of the court wore ribbons of foreign orders, put across one shoulder, and fastened down on the opposite side, as in the portraits of Queen Victoria; the Empress had a Spanish order, but seldom wore it, though it is seen in a large official portrait, copies of which were sent to provincial town halls, etc. She is represented in full court dress, with a train of green velvet, her Spanish order of violet-colored ribbon, and her high tiara of pearls and diamonds, the weight of which fatigued her so much that she disliked wearing it, though it was very becoming to her.

The (Princesse) Comtesse de Tascher de la Pagerie wore the ribbon and cross of Thérèse of Bavaria, and, in addition, the cross of the honorary canonesses of Remiremont (an order now extinct), which was given, in former times, only to those who could prove, on both father's and mother's lines, sixteen quarterings or generations of the highest nobility, an order whose abbesses were always princesses of the royal family of France.

The Duchesse de Tascher wore the ribbon and "Starred Cross" of Austria, which requires also a wonderful length of uninterrupted pedigree. With her magnificent figure and stately demeanor, she looked very grand on great court occasions, when she wore the blue satin train, with the ribbon and cross belonging to her order. Young unmarried ladies were not admitted on what were called "jours de manteau de cour"[1] (train days), so her daughters and myself begged her to rehearse before us the grand court courtesy, with the management of the long train, which was a very difficult matter, especially with the hooped skirts of the period, but which she performed so perfectly as to be

---

[1] Limited to the solemn receptions of the New Year, like the drawing-rooms of Queen Victoria.

celebrated for her manner of going through the ordeal.

The slow plunge downward to the very ground, with the head and figure erect; the still slower, and difficult, rise, without the slightest jerk; the graceful motion of the foot, to settle the train, avoiding any sudden kick backward; and the majestic gliding away, showing neither haste nor hurry—such a feat would require the practice of a lifetime to be performed with ease and grace, and was the triumph of aristocracy over "parvenues."

The ladies belonging to the court were obliged to wear the train on various state occasions, but others really had but one opportunity, that of the New Year's reception. The dress was very expensive, and was useless anywhere else, so the number of those attending these receptions gradually diminished every year, as they conferred no privilege with regard to court invitations.

The spring always brought a sort of deliverance to the Empress, who, during the winter months, could not conveniently take the air except in a carriage.

The Emperor finally inclosed a portion of the garden, and of the terrace bordering the river, for the use of his son and occasionally for himself; but the space was so narrow and so devoid of privacy that the Empress seldom took advantage of it. The little Prince habitually went in his carriage, with his escort, to "Bagatelle," a residence with grounds, situated in the Bois de Boulogne, which belonged to the Marquis of Hertford, where he played freely with his little friend Conneau, his habitual companion, son of the Emperor's physician and old friend, who had prepared his escape from the fortress of Ham. The Emperor had vainly tried to buy "Bagatelle" from Lord Hertford, but the latter was bound by a promise made to the Duchesse de Berry, mother of the Comte de Chambord, from whom he had purchased it with the condition that he would not sell it, and that she could redeem it at pleasure.

Consequently, Lord Hertford could only beg the Emperor to use it freely, and his kindness was accepted for the benefit of the Prince Imperial.

When the season was over, it was a relief to the imperial family to seek the country residences, where large parks gave them comparative liberty. Usually the spring brought them to Fontainebleau, an immense and splendid palace, with extensive grounds, and the beautiful forest so noted for its picturesque scenery.

Before leaving the Tuileries the Empress, with her dress protected by a black silk apron, and assisted by one of her attendant gentlemen, put away herself, with housewifely care, all the valuable china and pretty ornaments of her rooms, also giving particular orders for the covering of her furniture, even of her walls, and thus leaving everything perfectly protected from any possible injury of dust or sun before quitting the palace.

All the repairs in the internal arrangement, not only of the imperial apartments, but also those of the whole household, were managed by the upholstery department, called "La Régie," whose rule was supreme, and often very inconvenient, as no strange workmen were admitted, and those employed by La Régie had skeleton keys, asking leave of no one before entering one's private apartments.

"We have orders from La Régie," was the reply to every remonstrance.

"But why did you not execute these repairs during our absence, instead of removing our chairs and tables just when we absolutely require them?"

"We had not received orders."

It was necessary, on temporarily leaving the palace for any time, to put away carefully in private receptacles all valuables or papers; for, if left in the imperial articles of furniture, the slightest apparent flaw would cause everything to be turned out and left to the mercy or inquisitiveness of servants, while repairs were being executed. There was no intention of prying or investigation in these proceedings, but merely utter indifference as to the consequences and the annoyance of the victims. No parcel of any importance could be removed from the palace without the authorization of La Régie — perhaps a necessary measure of precaution to prevent imperial or national property from being disposed of by unscrupulous officials.

With regard to the proceedings of La Régie,

I can quote my own experience, having literally had all my furniture removed, and being left to stand in the empty room without a seat till I begged two chairs from my neighbor in the palace, the Archbishop of Bourges.

In the beginning of my stay at the Tuileries, on returning with the de Tascher family after an interval of absence, I was roused to considerable indignation on finding that the bureau in which I had locked all my private letters and papers had been taken away for trifling repairs, and the contents tumbled out, so that any one might read all that had been left there. I was so angry that on going to the Duchesse de Bassano, whose kindness encouraged me to frequent visits in her apartments, I could not help expressing my vexation at the petty annoyances of the administration of the palace; but she told me that she was not more privileged than I was myself, and quoted instances of what she had to endure in the way of such provoking measures, adding that before leaving the palace she always put her letters and papers in large sealed envelopes, as the only way of insuring safety.

I remember once going through a complete siege for three days, when I was alone at the Tuileries, being determined to keep out La Régie till the day of my own departure. I had not accompanied the family on this occasion. Being far from well in health, the waters of Spa, in Belgium, had been ordered for me; and it had been settled that I should accept the kindly offered protection of the Princess S—— (who was going there for her own health), and that I should spend three weeks there. I had naturally prepared suitable dresses for the occasion, and everything was laid out, ready for packing, when an authoritative knock at the door was heard at nine o'clock in the morning.

"What is the matter?"

"La Régie."

"Good Heavens! what does La Régie want?"

"We have to remove the furniture — to take up the carpets — and to wax the floors."

"But you have to attend to the apartments of the whole family; why must you begin with my rooms?"

"Our orders are to begin here."

I had only partially opened my door, which I closed at once with a peremptory refusal; and by another exit I flew to the quarters of the head upholsterer, who was in bed with the influenza, and could not be seen. I negotiated, however, with his housekeeper, and forcibly brought her to my rooms, of which I had taken the key. When she saw my preparations, her Frenchwoman's heart was touched, and admitting that it would be a great pity to spoil my arrangements, she returned to mediate with her master, coming back triumphantly with a three days' truce, granted to me on condition that I should "*defend myself*, and not allow any one to come in."

Consequently I remained with locked doors, stoutly resisting all attacks, and parleyed with the servant, who attended on me, before opening the door to allow him to bring in my meals.

On the third day of siege, in the morning, a knock came. Very angry at the perseverance shown I called sharply through the key-hole:

"I have told you again and again that I will not let you in. It is of no use to persist in this way; you shall not come in, and I will not open the door."

A laughing voice answered:

"Is that the way you receive the visits of your friends?"

"Why, who is there?"

"The Prince de Beauvau."

"Oh, good heavens, Prince!" I exclaimed, and opened the door to my visitor, who was immensely amused, saying that he had found the doors open, everything topsy-turvy, and no servants at hand; so he had come straight to my rooms, as he required some information from me, and had met with a very unexpected reception.

When the war with Austria for the liberation of Italy was declared, and the Empress appointed Regent, the court after the departure of the Emperor went to St. Cloud, and the usual visit to Fontainebleau was consequently omitted. The Empress took her new duties in earnest, holding three councils every week, of which two were at the Tuileries; but the distance from St. Cloud is trifling.

The destruction of St. Cloud (by the Prussians) is perhaps still more to be lamented than that of the Tuileries. It was a beautiful palace, with everything that could make a summer residence delightful, not too large, and of particularly graceful architecture and proportions. Withal, it was so conveniently near to Paris, that the sovereign was always within easy reach of the ministers and other functionaries who required to see him.

Within a reasonable walk from St. Cloud, through the long shady avenues of the park, was a small country-house called "Villeneuve l'Étang," which the Emperor had given to the Empress, who liked to play the part of Marie Antoinette, and had established a Swiss dairy in imitation of hers, but of more really rustic appearance than that of Trianon. The grounds were prettily laid out rather in the same style, and some charming "garden parties," as they would now be called, had been given there. The house was not remarkable in any way; but the principal room had furniture, dating from the First Empire, which had been entirely embroidered by Josephine and her ladies; the initial of her name, formed by small pink roses interlaced as a monogram, was worked on a ground of white silk with pretty effect.

The absence of the Emperor prevented all festivities at Villeneuve l'Étang or elsewhere; but we often walked in the shady avenues leading to it, or in the lovely garden nearer to the palace, which was devoted to the especial use of the Prince Imperial, then three years old.

We were invited to meet him at a breakfast, or rather collation, prepared for him by his state governess, Madame l'Amirale Bruat, "Gouvernante des Enfants de France." The little Prince, of course a mere baby, was accompanied by his English nurse, known as "Miss Shaw," a perfect specimen of the ruler of a nursery among the British aristocracy. She had no easy task in defending the child from the too exuberant endearments of the young ladies present, and energetically protested in English, that they were "worrying him and frightening him." The little Prince, of course, spoke English perfectly, having learned the language from her; but it was remarked, as a curious instance of childish instinct and of tact worthy of riper years, that nothing could induce him to speak English when any French were present.

When the nurse had extricated the little Prince from his too numerous admirers, he stood in the circle, silent and evidently shy, a pale, grave child, with large, earnest, blue eyes and brown curls, in a very simple white frock. I was standing a little aloof from the crowd pressing round him, but, to my surprise, he looked toward me with a fixed gaze, probably because I had let him alone.

The English nurse followed his eyes, saying immediately: "You like that lady, my Prince? Go to her." He came toward me, holding out his little hand and still looking at me intently. The nurse then said: "Get her a flower; go, get her a flower." He started off, and soon came back, holding a rose. Of course there was a rush to have it, but he held it high above his head, refusing to give the flower, and, running to where I stood, very gracefully handed it to me.

I have kept the faded leaves of that rose, withered like the budding hopes which then surrounded that little royal head.

The great treat which had been provided for him on this occasion was a play, performed by puppets that gave vent to all sorts of flattery concerning his "illustrious parents," with allusions to the war, and the glory of his family, all of which must have been incomprehensible even to a royal baby only three years old. He was seated in an arm-chair in front of the spectators, and was quiet for some time, evidently expecting that something was coming; but, after showing a considerable amount of patience, he could endure the trial no longer, and looking round with a most diverting expression of absolute astonishment, he energetically exclaimed:

"But this play is *not at all* amusing!"

There was a general laugh, and the little Prince was liberated from such wearisome pleasures.

He was at that time an unusually grave child;

but, as he grew older, boyish mischief had its turn, and he became as noisy as any others of his own age.

He was always extremely fond of everything belonging to the army; the great interest of his little life lay in changes of guards and regiments, their music, their flags and drums; and his delight was great when he was allowed to wear a military uniform himself. When he was naughty, he was told that he "disgraced his uniform," and this was more efficacious than ordinary punishment.

Like most young children, he disliked eating soup, and to induce him to take it, he was told that he must eat soup "to make him grow." He pondered over this assertion, and submitted to the soup as a necessity; but, some time afterward, seeing a tall grenadier mounting guard, the child stood before him, gazing at him with his grave, earnest eyes. Finally he said to him, with deep conviction in his tone:

"You must have eaten a great quantity of soup!"

When, after the victory of Solferino, there was a solemn "Te Deum" of thanksgiving at Notre Dame, it was considered advisable for the little Prince to accompany the Empress, who attended in state; but there was some anxiety as to the possibility of keeping such a young child quiet during the ceremony.

However, he behaved with exemplary gravity, and on returning to St. Cloud informed his governess that he "wanted another 'Te Deum,'" a wish which awakened a general echo. But hostilities were immediately ended by the Treaty of Villafranca.

The General Comte de Tascher had said to me at the beginning of the war:

"My experience of the wars of the First Empire has proved to me that everything depends on the first encounter. If our men are then victorious, the campaign will be successful from first to last; but the French cannot stand defeat, and once disheartened, nothing more can be done with them."

The truth of this appreciation became painfully evident during the Franco-German war. Happily, the Italian campaign began with victories.

CHAPTER X

The great review — Canrobert — MacMahon — The Zouaves — The flag with the ribbon and cross of the Legion of Honor — Violent rush of the crowd — I owe my life to Robert de Tascher — Court starvation on gala days.

THE Emperor's return was anxiously expected, and I can still vividly recall the sensation in the chapel at the palace of St. Cloud, when "L'Empereur!" was announced just before the mass began, and he appeared in the gallery, having arrived during the night, looking much bronzed by the Italian sun, but grave and calm as usual.

After the Emperor's return, I accompanied the Duchesse de Tascher and her elder daughter to see the great review of the troops in the Place Vendôme, a splendid sight which left a lasting impression on my mind and memory. We had seats in the space reserved for the household, next to the crimson velvet awning prepared for the Empress and her suite, opposite to the spot where the Emperor was stationed on horseback, beneath the column bearing the statue of the First Emperor. The whole of the Place Vendôme was filled with tiers of seats, rising one above another to the first floors of the houses, and forming a complete arena, where the troops, arriving by the Rue de la Paix, turned round the column and passed before the Emperor and Empress.

Scarcely had we taken our seats, when the Duc de Tascher came to us, sent by the Empress to fetch his wife and daughter, whom she wished to have with her. I remained therefore under the care of the Duke's son, Comte Robert de Tascher.

The heat was so intense that I felt inclined to envy the shade of the awning which protected the imperial party! The Emperor was before us, however, motionless on his horse, in the glaring sun, of which we really had as little as possible.

The whole scene was rather theatrical, but stirring and impressive in the greatest degree. As the regiments passed us, amidst the shouts of the spectators, the vacant places were left in the lines, showing the losses sustained—a sad sight. But the excitement was so great that everything was forgotten in the enthusiasm of the present hour, as each regiment was greeted by name with loud cries and applause. As the flags passed, burned and pierced by the shots received, every one felt electrified.

Suddenly a shout arose:

"Canrobert! Canrobert!"

And the Marshal appeared on a prancing horse, waving his sword with his usual rather theatrical air, while the cries of "Vive Canrobert!" rose

MARSHAL CASNOBERT.
FROM A PHOTOGRAPH BY LADREY-DISDERI.

MARSHAL MACMAHON.
FROM A PHOTOGRAPH BY LADREY-DISDERI.

louder and louder, as he passed before the Emperor, and a profusion of flowers fell around him.

"MacMahon! MacMahon!"

The hero of Magenta rode quietly forward,—a perfect gentleman and a perfect horseman, shown even by the manner in which he held his bridle, the hand seemed so sure, so firm and steady. He was evidently vexed and disconcerted by the commotion which his appearance caused, and persistently looked down, without seeming to accept the popular enthusiasm as addressed to himself personally. A wreath was thrown, which fell over his head down to his shoulders; he seemed to feel that he was being made ridiculous, and tore it off hastily, putting it over his horse's neck before him. MacMahon was by nature shy and unpretending; on this occasion he was evidently very anxious to get over the ordeal of the honors showered upon him.

"Les Zouaves! Les Zouaves!"

There was a thundering shout, and the Zouaves, who had scaled the seemingly inaccessible heights of Solferino, thereby deciding the fate of the battle, came proudly forward, bearing high their flag, a mere remnant clinging to the staff, proving through what a struggle the glorious emblem had been carried on to victory. The whole regiment having deserved the reward of the Legion of Honor, the flag bore the red ribbon and cross — but alas! how few followed it to share the hard-won glory! Nevertheless, the sight was not to be forgotten, and no one could help sharing the general enthusiasm. The old Comte de Tascher, however, who had seen the victories of the first Napoleon, looked grave and anxious when I spoke to him of the stirring scene. The Countess, in answer to my warm congratulations, said:

"The Emperor is wonderfully fortunate in all he undertakes—*too* fortunate. A day must come when all this will be reversed."

Happily, neither saw that fatal day when it came, as they predicted.

As if to foreshadow the future, a tremendous storm burst over us before the glorious review was ended, and Robert de Tascher hastily led me under the shelter of one of the houses behind us (for the rain poured in torrents), to the great indignation of an old gentleman near us, who declared that it was perfectly disgraceful to see women thinking only of their clothes, when the Emperor, who was being drenched to the skin before us, was motionless on his horse.

The downpour was, however, of short duration, and we were able to return to our seats. But when all was over, and we left the Place Vendôme, although we had prudently waited till our exit seemed perfectly safe, there was a fearful and unexpected rush of the crowd in the Rue Castiglione to see the Empress, and I certainly owed my life on that occasion to the physical vigor and cool presence of mind shown by Comte Robert de Tascher, with whom I finally reached the Tuileries, where I was to meet my elder pupil, who returned with me to St. Cloud, the Duke and Duchess having to attend the court banquet. We had left at half-past seven in the morning, and did not get back till the same hour of the evening. Of course refreshments had been prepared for the Empress, and those who accompanied her were able to partake of them; but I could have literally nothing, and when I reached the Tuileries (all our own cookery department being at St. Cloud), nothing was to be had but one or two small cakes, which Robert de Tascher managed to procure for me, and which constituted my sole support for twelve hours. But such inconveniences are of frequent occurrence in court life.

CHAPTER XI

Paris in the early days of the Second Empire — Diplomatic changes after the Italian war — A great name — A young ambassadress — Eccentricities of the Princess Metternich — Her imprudence and morbid curiosity — Anecdotes — A "real" Empress — Practical joke on a lady-in-waiting — Dispute with Madame de Persigny — Why the Princess Metternich could not yield to her — Count Sandor — His strange exploits — Practical joke on his old housekeeper — Imperial hospitality at Compiègne — Dresses required for the week's visit — Daily life of the visitors — Kindness of the Imperial hosts — Five o'clock tea in the private apartments of the Empress — Evenings — Questionable diversions provided by the Princess Metternich — Exaggerated reports — Personal description of the Princess Metternich — General Fleury.

AFTER the Italian war, there were necessarily important changes in the great diplomatic posts, and Baron von Hübner (best known to the general public by his interesting travels, which show considerable acuteness of observation), was replaced at the Austrian embassy by Prince Richard Metternich.

A great historical name is often an inconvenient inheritance, by raising too great expectations; and the agreeable, well-bred Austrian gentleman who bore this title was certainly not equal to those which it awakened. He was soon better known by his wife's eccentricities than by his own merits.

Too young in every respect for such a position as that of ambassadress, the Princess Metternich soon attracted unfavorable notice by her strange ways and fancies, which first astonished Parisian society, and then provoked severe criticism.

The Princess Metternich was a mere wayward, spoiled child, who imagined that her high rank authorized her to defy all rules of decorum; and that, so long as she abstained from what was absolutely wicked, she could do anything she pleased.

At that time there was a sort of intoxication in the very atmosphere of Paris, a fever of enjoyment—a passion for constant amusement, for constant excitement, and, amongst women, for extravagance of dress. This was encouraged by the court, with the intention of giving an impetus to trade, and of gaining popularity by favoring constant festivities and consequently constant expense. In the days of Louis Philippe there had been great moderation in all matters of luxury; the King and Queen were aged, sensible and economical; the young princesses were kept within rigid bounds by the example above them. But when the Emperor came to the throne, after a period of revolution and consequent commercial stagnation, he wished to revive trade, and also to give the prestige of splendor to a court which so many did not seem to take in earnest. His beautiful wife, suddenly raised to a supreme position for which nothing in her previous life had prepared her, finding what seemed unlimited means within her reach, keenly enjoyed the possibility of procuring everything that pleased her, and enhanced her remarkable personal attractions by all the advantages of exquisite toilette without consideration of cost. Everything that she wore suited her admirably; others tried to imitate her, and the general tone became raised. She had the art of constantly choosing something new and unusual, which attracted attention, so that, instead of being satisfied with conventional types of silks and satins, which formerly had been considered sufficient for all occasions, every one tried to invent something different from others, and to improve upon what had been seen before. Consequently, not only in dress, but in all matters of taste and luxury, there was an eager struggle to outvie others, to reach a higher degree of splendor, and extravagance became universal. Paris was a sort of fairyland, where every one lived only for amusement, and where every one seemed rich and happy. What lay underneath all this, would not bear close examination — the dishonorable acts of all kinds, which too often were needed to produce the glamour deceiving superficial observers.

Into this hotbed of "pomps and vanities" came the young and thoughtless Princess Metternich, with all the pride characterizing the high aristocracy of her native land, and fully disposed both to enjoy, and to despise, what awaited her. She had been accustomed to the restricted society of

Vienna, composed of distinct circles, wheels within wheels according to rank and social privileges, those belonging to each circle keeping aloof from all others, marrying only amongst their equals, and associating exclusively together. As a natural consequence, the quintessence of the aristocracy, forming the most limited among these circles, becomes a sort of large family; all are more or less related to each other; all are intimate from childhood. In such a society, the hoydenish ways of "Pauline" were only smiled at, and were not of much consequence. But when she came to a cosmopolitan city like Paris, full of observant enemies, who did not care in the least for her quarterings, or her faultless pedigree, and did not admit any superiority, the case was very different. Her husband ought to have understood this, and to have interposed his authority; but he was indolently indifferent, and when his wife exceeded all social limits, the strongest reproof was a languid, "Aber, Pauline!" which in no way acted as a check.

In the Princess Metternich was an inexplicable mixture of innate high breeding and acquired tastes of lower degree. When she appeared in society, at her very entrance there could be no mistake: from head to foot, she was the high-born lady, the *grande dame*. And yet she had an extraordinary inclination for walking on the edges of moral quagmires, and peeping into them, with a proud conviction that her foot could never slip. There are stories of her imprudent adventures; but she escaped unscathed, and had no other motive in seeking them than curiosity — foolish, morbid curiosity — as to people and matters which should never have been even mentioned in her presence. She acted with a degree of rashness and folly which would have ruined most women; yet no one ever really attacked her reputation; all allowed that, according to the expression of a lady of the court, she had never "crossed the Rubicon."

Notwithstanding all her follies, the Princess Metternich was far from being silly: on the contrary, she had considerable wit, and great sharpness of repartee. As she did not care for anything she said, her retorts were often very clever, and always amusing, but too free to be easily repeated. She affected masculine manners. When she first arrived in France she had been invited to Compiègne, with other ladies of the "corps diplomatique," and on their return in the train, Lord Cowley, then British ambassador, asked if he might be indulged in a cigarette. The young ambassadress drew from her pocket a cigar-case of most masculine appearance, offered him a formidable cigar, and took one herself.

Some time afterward a lady of my acquaintance called on the ambassadress of Austria. The majordomo informed her that "her Highness" was in the garden. The Comtesse de L—— stepped into the garden, looking about her wonderingly in search of the Princess, when a voice, seeming to come from on high, called to her. She looked up: the ambassadress was lying on her back, in a hammock slung among the trees, smoking a cigar.

Her will alone seemed to her so sufficient to justify her acts that, haughty as she was, she did not hesitate to invite to her dinner-table the celebrated "Thérésa," a singer whom no one else, at that time, would have dared to receive, and yet from whom the Princess Metternich condescended to take lessons, in order to sing her bold songs with duly pointed emphasis.

The mischief done by the example of the Princess Metternich in Parisian society is indescribable. She threw down the barrier which hitherto had separated respectable women from those who were not, and led the way to a liberty of speech and liberty of action which were unknown before. She was much attached to her husband, and, in essentials, she was a good wife; others, less favorably situated, may not have escaped, as she did, from the natural consequences of looking too closely over the frontier of the Debatable Land. It is not unlikely that the excessive pride of the Princess Metternich may have led her to imagine that in Paris she might do anything without compromising her dignity. She was intimate with a lady who, although received everywhere in Parisian society, did not seem to be sufficiently her equal in rank to become her friend. To a remark on the subject, she carelessly answered: "Oh, it is all very well *here*—of course, I could not see her in Vienna!"

She was reported to have made a more impertinent speech at Compiègne while on a visit there. The short, looped-up skirts were just beginning to be worn; the Empress had not yet habitually adopted them, and the Princess Metternich had been urging her to appear thus dressed on the public occasion of the races in the town, against the opinion of her ladies. When the Empress left the room, one of the ladies-in-waiting said to the Princess:

"Would you give the same advice to *your* Empress?"

"Oh, no," said the Princess; "but the case is quite different—the Empress Elizabeth is a *real* Empress."

I have no positive information as to the absolute trustworthiness of this report; but it was not unlike the style of the Princess Metternich, and was currently repeated.

On another occasion at Compiègne, in the presence of the Empress, on a rainy day, which had brought some dullness to the circle, the Princess Metternich, by way of diversion, suddenly seized one of the ladies-in-waiting, tripped her up in school-boy fashion, and laid her flat on her back prostrate on the floor. This was told to me by an eye-witness of the scene, which shocked every one present, the more so as the victim chosen, the Comtesse de M——, was particularly lady-like, quiet, and unoffending.

The Empress was never really intimate with the Princess Metternich, but she liked her, on the whole, and her oddities amused her, so she was always a welcome guest, especially in the country-residences, such as Fontainebleau and Compiègne, where invitations were greatly extended, and where the "series," as they were called, of about eighty visitors at a time, for a week's stay, rendered amusement for all an arduous task to the kind imperial hosts.

The hospitality of Fontainebleau and Compiègne, but particularly the latter, was dispensed in the most liberal manner, and nothing was neglected that could make the guests enjoy the visit, which, however, was perhaps too much prolonged for pleasure, on both sides. The invitations were for a week, but those particularly favored were requested to remain for another "series"; the fatigue was excessive, and every one felt surprise that the Empress could continue such a life for several weeks.

In the spring the court went to Fontainebleau, but the invitations were of a less general kind, and were confined more to those in some way connected with the court itself, and considered as friends. There were also foreign princes and the members of their embassies; but the style was more exclusive than at Compiègne, where every one of any note was invited at least once. Painters, composers, literary men, were included in the "series." Their wives generally did not accompany them, and the masculine costume requiring no variety, they were able to enjoy the imperial hospitality without too much expense; but to those in a more aristocratic position, whose wives must necessarily appear, Compiègne entailed ruinous consequences. It was understood that no dress could be worn more than once; for a week's stay it was usual, therefore, to take fifteen dresses, seven of which were intended for the evening, and consequently must be of the most expensive kind. The extravagance of Compiègne caused so much blame that the Empress, who at first had encouraged, by her example, the follies of those around her, tried to restrain them by adopting for drives and walks in the forest a plain skirt of black silk over a red woolen or tartan underskirt; but this only caused additional complications. The weather in November was not always favorable, and the costume was only fit for out-door wear. Then came the hunts of Compiègne, so splendidly organized; those who followed on horseback wore the hunting uniform of green cloth, trimmed with gold lace and crimson velvet, very handsome, but necessarily expensive.

There were four successive "series" of invitations for Compiègne; the guests of each "series" went together in a special train prepared for the occasion, followed by innumerable trunks containing the dresses provided for the week.

At the Compiègne station the imperial carriages awaited the guests, taking them through the town to the palace, which was brilliantly lighted up to receive them, as the hour of arrival was late in the afternoon, and the season November. On reaching the palace, a splendid vestibule was first crossed between two rows of servants in the imperial livery; the Prefect of the Palace then came forward to receive the guests, assigning to each group a servant, who led the way to the apartments prepared for them, which were as comfortable and convenient as possible. Everything looked cheerful and encouraging to new-comers, who were often rather nervous as to the trial before them.

Shortly after seven, the guests assembled in the great drawing-room to await the entrance of the Emperor and Empress, who spoke to those known to them, and then led the way together into the immense dining-hall, where the dinner was served in splendid state. A band played during dinner, after which their Majesties rose, and followed by the guests, returned to the drawing-room. The great difficulty of amusing, during a whole week, eighty strangers of different ranks in society (many of whom knew nothing of court usage), may be imagined. The Emperor and Empress tried to speak to every one with the greatest kindness and simplicity of manner, begging them to feel perfectly at home, to consider themselves free to abstain from any excursion if they preferred not to join the others, to do exactly as they pleased with regard to the disposal of the day; but naturally every one felt that this indulgence could not be interpreted too literally. The days were spent in drives through the forest in open carriages, which all did not enjoy in November; the celebrated staghunts of Compiègne, followed in carriages or on horseback at pleasure; shooting-parties with the Emperor, etc. At five o'clock the most noted among those present—literary men, artists, and scientific celebrities—were invited to take tea in the private apartment of the Empress, who then kindly and with much tact tried to draw out each one by leading the conversation to the particular subjects in which they had reached fame. These conversations, which were full of interest to those who were admitted by privilege, delighted the Empress so much that she forgot the hour, and often did not give the signal of departure till seven o'clock, a cause of intense anxiety to those who, having probably a considerable distance to go before reaching their apartments, were yet obliged to be punctually ready in full dress before half-past seven, when their Majesties made their appearance before dinner.

The evenings were the most trying part of the day here as elsewhere. The Princess Metternich was then of immense resource in all the entertainments prepared by the court. She sang and acted cleverly; she danced as if she had been trained for the ballet; she got up charades, plays, "tableaux vivants," in short, anything that was required, with a spirit and animation which never flagged.

But matters did not always go on smoothly; there were differences of view and of opinion, and the Princess then became much excited.

On one occasion of this kind there was a memorable dispute with Madame de Persigny, wife of the well-known statesman, who was herself equally well known for her caprices of temper. Though by no means sufficiently witty to be a match for the sharp tongue of the Princess Metternich, she was quite able by her obstinacy to destroy the effect of all the plans of her opponent. The Princess, though by nature far more good-humored than Madame de Persigny, at last having completely lost patience, appealed to the Empress, who, much annoyed at the dispute, was trying in vain to restore peace:

"Pray, pray, my dear Princess, let the matter rest! spare her — remember that her mother is mad!"

"So her mother is mad?" retorted the Princess. "Well, Madame, my father is mad; so why should I give in to her?"

The argument was irresistible, and the Empress could not help laughing; but the manner in which the Princess had honored her father's peculiarities was received in general with more amusement than approbation.

Count Sandor, the father of the Princess Metternich, was noted for his eccentricities and wonderful adventures. He was a remarkable horseman, and performed all sorts of apparently impossible feats on horseback, risking his life at each one, and escaping by what seemed a miracle, or rather a succession of miracles; though not without serious injuries, some of which had affected his brain, according to public rumor.

A collection of drawings representing these strange performances had been engraved and bound in a volume, and I had an opportunity of examining this series of crack-brained exploits and hair-breadth escapes. One of the most amusing though really the most pitiable of the former, represented his houskeeper, a fat old woman, with an agonized expression of fright on her upturned face, held horizontally by two men, while her master leaped his horse backward and forward over her. The poor creature was evidently terrified out of her senses, and no wonder.

The Princess Metternich had no beauty; her face was of absolutely simian type, only redeemed by bright intelligent eyes; her complexion was dark, her mouth was large, and her nose was flat." Even her figure was more than slender, and devoid of all beauty of form; but owing to her remarkable elegance of demeanor, her animated expression of countenance, and her richly fashionable dress, she was considered attractive, notwithstanding her physical disadvantages.

She was passionately fond of dress, and in this, as in all things, her taste led her into eccentricity regardless of expense. At the Austrian embassy, her

EMPRESS EUGÉNIE, 1863.
FROM A PHOTOGRAPH BY GEORGES SPRINGER.

rooms, furniture, receptions, carriages, and horses were only surpassed by the court, and her example had a pernicious influence on the general mania for extravagance of all kinds.

The turnout of the Emperor's carriages, horses, and liveries was unsurpassed in Europe, under the direction of General Fleury, who was more remarkable in this respect than as a military commander. In fact, he would probably never have reached such high promotion had he not been the friend of the Emperor, and his auxiliary in the "coup d'état," when he was only Captain Fleury at the Élysée. He was neither liked nor much esteemed in general; but he certainly performed admirably his duties as "Grand Écuyer," or what at the English court would be termed "Master of the Horse."

The Emperor and Empress were the kindest of hosts, most anxious to amuse their guests and to make their visits as pleasant as possible; therefore the Princess Metternich was welcome, because she brought with her life and animation; but at the same time her performances were open to criticism with regard to their deficiency in that refinement and social propriety which should be guarded carefully in such a circle, thus gradually drawing on the Empress to show too much indulgence when amused. Unfortunately, in addition to the dubious songs, charades, and plays got up by the Princess Metternich, romping games were often chosen as a diversion: which, though certainly undignified and ill suited to those beyond school years, had not, however, the character attributed to them by public report, nor the licentious freedom believed in by the "Faubourg St. Germain," and so contemptuously sneered at by its aristocratic inhabitants.

The mistake lay in doing on a large scale what ought to be tolerated only among intimate friends and very young people. But the mean ingratitude of those who enjoyed all the generous kindness lavished on their guests by the imperial hosts, and then disfigured the truth to sneer at them with their enemies, was too contemptible to be even mentioned with patience.

CHAPTER XII

"Golden wedding" of the Comte and Comtesse de Tascher de la Pagerie — Curious story of a lost ring — Marriage of my elder pupil — Prince Maximilian von Thurn und Taxis — Death of the Comte de Tascher — Kindness and affectionate attentions of the Emperor and Empress during his last illness — Sorrow of the Emperor — The Count laid out in state — Effect on the Empress — Her nervous condition — Her private sorrows — She begins to interfere in political matters — Our home life after the death of the Comte de Tascher — Home evenings — Weekly receptions — Ambassadors Extraordinary from Oriental lands — The Persian Ambassador — The Embassy from Siam — Reception at Fontainebleau — The hair-dresser Leroy.

THE year that followed the war with Austria (the fourth of my residence at the palace of the Tuileries) was marked by a family event, the "golden wedding," or fiftieth anniversary of the marriage of the Comte and Comtesse de Tascher de la Pagerie, which was celebrated at Baden-Baden in the presence of all their children and grandchildren.

A curious circumstance occurred on this occasion, which is worthy of mention. The (Princess) Comtesse de Tascher had lost, many years before, her wedding-ring, to her great distress, and it had never been found. Shortly before the festivities of the "golden wedding," the Duchess of Hamilton, on looking over the jewelry left by her mother, the Grand-Duchess of Baden, whose death had occurred during the preceding winter, found a small packet labeled: "The wedding-ring of Amélie von der Leyen, sold by a Jew-peddler as having belonged to the Empress Joséphine: to be returned." It was evident that the Grand-Duchess, who was the most absent-minded of women, had put this away carefully and entirely forgotten it. The Duchess of Hamilton, seeing the inscription engraved inside: "L. Tascher de la Pagerie*— A. von der Leyen,"—with the date of their marriage, sent it to the Count with the above explanation. He kept the matter secret till the "golden wedding," when the ring which had been lost for so long was again placed on the finger of Amélie von der Leyen on the fiftieth anniversary of the marriage which had taken place under such sad circumstances.

I was much moved on this occasion by the kindness of the old Count, who called me to him, saying: "My dear, in commemoration of my fiftieth wedding-day I have had rings made *for all my children, and here is yours.*" I have always worn it since, and kept it as a precious memorial.

* The Empress Joséphine having adopted the habit of signing her name "Tascher de la Pagerie," *without* the "de," the family followed her example till the title of Duke, attached to the name of Tascher, obliged them to resume the "de." The title was "Duc de Tascher," and not "de la Pagerie," an addition to the name which merely served to distinguish the elder branch from the younger, called simply "de Tascher."

The "golden wedding" was closely followed by the marriage of my elder pupil, Eugénie de Tascher de la Pagerie, with H. S. H. Prince Maximilian von Thurn und Taxis, thus adding other royal alliances to those which already distinguished the family of de Tascher de la Pagerie. One of the Princes von Thurn und Taxis married an archduchess of Austria; another, a princess of Bavaria, sister to the Empress Elizabeth. The marriage with Prince Maximilian, who, withal, was remarkably handsome and of most princely exterior, could only be very agreeable to the whole family, and brought much happiness to the young bride.

Alas! this joyful event was followed by a great affliction—the death of her dear grandfather, a few months later, for whom I mourned as if I had indeed been one of his children.

The Emperor and Empress visited him constantly during his illness, the Empress herself undertaking various small cares of the sick-room, as a daughter might have done. The Emperor was deeply moved when he saw that the end was at hand; the tears, which he could not repress, were running down his face, as he stood by the bed of his old and faithful friend. I was much struck by the gentleness of his manner and the softness of his voice, in great contrast with the somewhat harsh tones of the Empress. Napoleon III. retained his hat, according to royal privilege, but it seemed strange under such circumstances; the Empress Eugénie wore nothing on her hair, and was in home toilette of mourning for her sister, the Duchess of Alva.

The death of the Comte de Tascher de la Pagerie was that of a sincere and fervent Christian, leaving memories of peace and religious hope to all who were present. The Duke, his son, replaced him in his court duties, but his title of "Grand Master" remained in abeyance.

The Emperor and Empress came together to visit his widow, and here a painful scene took place. The Count was laid out in state, and according to German custom, all visitors were at once shown into his room. This was quite unexpected by the Empress, who was so startled and shocked that she fell into violent hysterics. She was carried immediately into a room belonging to one of the ladies of the family, who hastened to offer their assistance, while the Emperor stood by helpless, like most men on such occasions, repeating: "My poor Eugénie!" in tones of consternation. But the annoyance caused by the consequences of such an unfortunate mistake left a painful impression on the mind of the Empress, and in some measure chilled her kind sympathy.

The death of her sister, the Duchess of Alva,* had thrown her into a very nervous and excitable state. At the same time she had serious domestic sorrows, into the cause of which the world was

---

* Called by the French: "Duchesse d'Albe."

only too completely initiated, but which she could not discuss with her ladies, while her sister was a natural confidante in the terrible moral isolation of her high position. The Duchess of Alva, more calm, perhaps more reasonable than the Empress Eugénie, had a soothing influence over her violent feelings and impulsive resolutions, to which she yielded without resistance after the death of her sister. Every one knew that her violent grief, her incessant weeping, had other causes besides her recent loss, although officially it was supposed to be the only one. The Emperor was gentle and kind as ever in his intercourse with her, but never seemed to understand the real motive of her persistent affliction, to which he attached no importance. He loved the wife whom he had chosen, in spite of all the opposition shown by his best friends; but he was too attentive to others, and very unscrupulously indulged his many fancies, as all knew; and to this his wife could never be resigned. She had not to endure the public insults which his predecessors inflicted on their consorts; but what took place in private was not the less known by the world, for monarchs live in a glass case, observed by all.

At this time the Empress began to take an interest in political matters, and it was thought advisable to humor her in this new fancy, as a means of diverting her mind from other problems to be solved of a more inconvenient kind. She had held the nominal office of Regent during the Italian war of 1859: as she might be called upon to do so again, she was now allowed to be present at the councils, and she began to interfere in matters concerning the affairs of State. This, again, was most unwelcome to the nation, always averse to female influence, and by no means willing to be governed by "Mademoiselle de Montijo." The nature of the Empress was particularly unfitted for political interference; she was essentially impulsive, vehement in the expression of her preferences or views, and easily worked upon by those who contrived to win her confidence. She was too sincere and straightforward herself to understand diplomatic intrigues, or to suspect secret motives; and thus she was unknowingly induced to favor the various private interests of those by whom France and Napoleon III. were drawn into the Mexican war, with its miserable results — the beginning of the Emperor's downward career. Unhappily, the Empress Eugénie continued to interfere in political questions, and ended by taking a passionate interest in public affairs. She was surrounded by flatterers, who made her their tool for the advantage of their own views, while she mistook her own high spirit and her visions of romantic heroism for the genius of a Maria Theresa or a Catherine. At first the Emperor resisted, and while assisted by his first supporters, Morny, Walewski, even Persigny, — who, though erratic, was at least energetic and devoted, —

he had his own way in what was essential; but, as these counselors died off, or retired from public affairs, and his own health became seriously affected, he yielded more and more to an ever-increasing yearning for domestic peace.

After the period of mourning which followed the death of the General Comte de Tascher, the family resumed with some modifications the life previously described. The (Princess) Countess, however, now left social duties more exclusively to her daughter-in-law, the Duchess, and only went out to the theaters and operas, still her favorite diversion, where I usually accompanied her. On other evenings visitors came; about nine o'clock a tea-table was brought in, where I presided, assisted by Mademoiselle de Tascher de la Pagerie and often by Mesdemoiselles de Bassano, who handed the cups, with the sugar-basin and cream-jug — a graceful French custom only modified for large parties, where servants perform the offices usually left to the daughters of the house and their young friends. These quiet evenings were made particularly agreeable by the animated conversation of the distinguished visitors — the *causerie* in which the French excel, and which here had full play. Once a week the Duchess held a large "reception," where all the fashionable society of the Empire came, and where first-rate amateurs and budding artistic celebrities played and sang, without the formality of a regular concert. These evenings were much enjoyed, for liberty reigned supreme: as several rooms were thrown open, the guests could walk about and converse freely, no one being obliged to listen to the music who did not care for it.

The arrival of ambassadors-extraordinary from Oriental lands brought some diversion to the monotony of the imperial court, which the Empress welcomed with delight. In those days a Sultan, or a Shah, did not show his sacred person in "giaour" regions, and but little was known of their distant countries, which seemed to belong to the world of the "Arabian Nights."

When the arrival of an ambassador from Persia was officially announced, the Empress Eugénie had but one thought, that of dazzling his Oriental mind by a wonderful display of European magnificence. Usually a Queen-Consort never appeared officially on such occasions; but the Empress decided that she would be present in state, with all her ladies around her in full court dress, which she would wear herself, with a profusion of jewels. Everything was settled according to her wishes; she was present at the reception of the Ambassador, seated in imperial state, and looked very beautiful, while all wondered how she would impress the Ambassador. When he retired, one of the French gentlemen who had escorted him into the imperial presence asked what he thought of the Empress.

"The Empress!" he exclaimed, with contemptuous astonishment. "I did not look at her. It is beneath my dignity to look at a woman. I only saw the Emperor."

This result of so much trouble taken was rather disconcerting for those concerned; but there was a good deal of suppressed laughter among the officials who had witnessed the ceremony.

The Embassy from Siam followed, described to us by the Bavarian minister as "a set of fellows in long silk dressing-gowns, looking as if they had been molded in greenish chocolate," and who were to bring to the Emperor the presents sent by the King of Siam, which they were to offer on their hands and knees. The Emperor, who had decided to receive them in the gallery of Henry II. at the palace of Fontainebleau, earnestly wished to dispense with this part of the ceremony; but he was told that he would only lose all majesty in their appreciation, and all claim to their respect.

The Empress was also present in full imperial state with her ladies around her; the latter had been particularly requested not to yield to any temptation to laugh during the performance; but the sight of human beings crawling on the floor like animals was so painful that no one felt any inclination even to smile. The unfortunate ambassador carried a large gold cup or basin containing the presents above his head, and was consequently obliged to use his elbows to work his way forward on his knees. When he reached the

throne, panting and gasping, the Emperor could
bear the sight no longer, but stepped down to
save him the ascent, taking the presents from him,
and raising him to his feet.

I remember seeing the Siamese, who were the
great "lions" of the day, at the opera, and thinking the description of the Bavarian minister very
graphic and accurate. The opera represented was
Félicien David's "Herculaneum," and the alarm of
the Siamese at the final conflagration was very
amusing to witness. They were, not unnaturally,
convinced that the theater was on fire, and insisted
on leaving the building, pointing to the stage with
the greatest terror, rushing to the door of the box,
and being most reluctantly brought back by the
French gentlemen who escorted them. They were
evidently much relieved when the curtain fell, and
they were allowed to retire.

On official occasions, such as the preceding, and
others, an important part in the preparations fell
to the share of a functionary who, though unnoticed, was not unknown — the hair-dresser of the
Empress, named Leroy. Of course all fashionable ladies wished to have their hair dressed by
Leroy; but on great occasions only those of very
high rank, or very prominent positions, could as-
pire to the care of the great man himself; all
others had to be satisfied with the skill of his
assistants. He was quite a character: a stout,
middle-aged man, who came in his carriage at the

hour he pleased (which had to be awaited during the whole day), and who, when he chose to come, rushed in like a conqueror, waving his comb, dressed in a brown linen oversuit, ordering the servants about, and desiring the presence of their mistress *immediately* — he could not be kept waiting. Duchesses and princesses, who had spent the day in white wrappers to be ready for his offices, then flew to their dressing-rooms with all due submission and alacrity. In two minutes their hair was disheveled on their shoulders, and with marvelous rapidity gathered up and arranged according to his taste and fancy, while he talked incessantly, principally of the Empress, lauding her to the skies, then reverting to Marie Antoinette and her hair-dresser; if *he* had filled that post, she would never have been guillotined. Oh, no! he would have found means to prevent that. He would guarantee that nothing would happen to the Empress Eugénie, etc., etc. Meanwhile the hair in his hands assumed beautiful shapes, and, as he put in the jewels, he would say proudly: "No fear of their coming out! No lady ever lost a diamond that *I* had fastened."

And truly they were wonderfully secure. The result of his rapid manipulations was always perfect, but it was dearly paid for by hours of waiting. I have seen the Duchesse de Tascher, with her hair dressed for a ball at eleven o'clock in the morning, sitting motionless during the whole day, so that nothing should be disturbed in her head-dress.

When the King of Prussia[1] visited Napoleon III. at Compiègne, the Empress, of course, considered the presence of Leroy indispensable, and he was summoned to Compiègne for the whole of the King's visit. But it so happened that some important wedding festivities at Berlin had caused lucrative offers to be addressed to Leroy, who explained the case to the Empress, imploring her to dispense with his services. Too kind to refuse, yet considerably vexed and engrossed by that one thought, the Empress went to the Emperor's private room, where he was deeply engaged in political cogitations caused by the visit of the King, and the matters to be discussed.

"Can you imagine anything more tiresome?" she said to the Emperor. "Here is Leroy, who has been apologizing and entreating my forgiveness, because he has been summoned to Berlin, and must go immediately."

The Emperor, to whom the sound "Leroy" could only mean "Le Roi" (the King), and who thought only of the King of Prussia, exclaimed in great alarm:

"*Le Roi!* summoned to Berlin! But this is most serious! How is it that I have not been informed? You say he is going immediately? What can have happened?"

[1] Afterward Emperor of Germany.

The Empress, surprised at the extreme interest shown by the Emperor in the proceedings of "Leroy," continued her lamentations; till at last, after considerable anxiety, Napoleon III. discovered that the important departure was that of her hairdresser.

CHAPTER XIII

The little Prince Imperial — The Emperor's excessive indulgence — Vain efforts of the Empress "to bring up that child properly"— The Empress and the pony — The Emperor and the orange — Amiable disposition of the Prince — His efforts to "earn money for the poor"— General Frossard's military discipline - Anecdotes — The "honor of the uniform" — The Prince takes the measles — Seriously ill — Nursed by the Empress with the greatest maternal devotion.

THE little Prince was now growing out of babyhood, and was really a most amiable and interesting child, although surrounded by adulation and obsequiousness to a degree which would have ruined most children. Happily his English nurse, Miss Shaw, whom he dearly loved, treated him with English good sense, and had an excellent influence over him. Others were also to be found who did not consider that they were bound to worship the Emperor's heir.

On one occasion he childishly failed in due decorum toward the Duc de Tascher, who took him sharply to task, pointing out in very plain terms the superiority of a man of his age and position over a "gamin" like himself. The child was immensely astonished, but fully understood the les-

THE PRINCE IMPERIAL.
FROM A PHOTOGRAPH BY LADREY-DISDERI.

son. The little Prince was spoiled to excess by his father; his mother naturally wished to counterbalance the latter's over-indulgence, but she was not always judicious in her energetic interference. One instance may be quoted among many. The very first time that the little Prince was seated on a pony as a mere baby of three years old, the equerry, M. Bâchon, was carefully holding him, and leading the pony step by step, when suddenly the Empress came up, indignantly declaring that she would not have such absurd petting, concluding with a cut of her whip to the pony, who started off. Bâchon, terrified, uttered an energetic expletive, succeeded in stopping the pony, and brought back the child unhurt; but he was too angry to remember official decorum, and expressed his feelings with an amount of vigor very unusual in courts, while the English nurse indulged in more respectful lamentations: "Oh! your Majesty! You should n't, your Majesty! You 've only *one*, you know!"

It is evident that the Empress in no way intended to risk the life of her child; but she was herself fearless to excess and often thoughtless in the presence of danger. She was determined that her son should not be a milk-sop, and she did not stop to examine the "fitness of things."

The Emperor, on the other hand, shrank from giving him pain to an almost absurd degree. The child was once playing with a small mandarin orange, which he tried to get into his mouth. The Emperor, alarmed, cried: "Take it from him! He will choke himself!" The Duc de Tascher took the orange forcibly from the child, not without resistance on his part, and laughingly rallied the Emperor on his not having done so himself. "I *could* not." the Emperor exclaimed; "he would not love me."

When the time came for putting him under the care of a tutor, one of the ladies de Tascher said to the child: "Ah, Monseigneur! now you will have to be obedient and to work hard at your lessons."

He gravely answered: "That is not so sure. Mama always says *no;* but then papa always says *yes,* and I have my own will besides; *that makes three.*"

Like most children, the little Prince had a great yearning for "grown-up pleasures," and hearing at Compiègne conversations on a new play which was to be acted there by the Comédie-Française, he immediately expressed an eager wish to be present. Comtesse Stéphanie de Tascher said at once: "No, no, Monseigneur; little boys go to bed, and do not go to plays."

He looked at her gravely, and in a very decided tone replied:

"We shall see. I will speak to papa about it."

And, of course, "papa" yielded, to the great annoyance of his mother, who disapproved.

The tutor had no easy task before him, and the Empress exclaimed in despair:

"It is impossible to bring up that child properly!"

Happily his disposition was excellent and easily worked upon; in more serious matters it was sufficient to tell him that the "honor of his uniform" was concerned, to obtain immediate submission.

The Emperor promised that his "good marks" from his tutor should be paid him in money for the poor, which was to be kept in a special box. When the "good marks" failed, he was reminded that the poor would suffer through his fault, and this was deeply felt by the child. When his box filled, his delight was pretty to witness; *he* had earned the money, and the poor people would have it. "Look at my box! See how much money I have got!" running in great glee to show it to the Comtesse Stéphanie de Tascher.

The little Prince was brought forward more than was desirable, owing to his father's excessive indulgence. When he was eight years old he was admitted to the imperial dinner-table. All those accustomed to children will understand how objectionable such an arrangement must have been for his health as well as for his proper education. At Compiègne he was allowed far too much participation in the pleasures provided for the guests; and when only nine years old he took a prominent part in an entertainment where the Princess Metternich and others performed. The little Prince sang songs composed for the occasion, with appropriate words, and filled his part in a very satisfactory and pleasing manner; but the whole was terribly misplaced for his health and his best interests, and all sensible people felt, like the Comtesse Stéphanie de Tascher, "that little boys ought to go to bed."

I remember seeing him at an official costume ball in the "Salle des Maréchaux," and the disapprobation of the (Princess) Countess, who was positively unhappy, and repeated: "How injudicious! Such a scene of excitement for such a young brain!"

On a similar occasion the little Prince caught the measles from a young lady who actually sacrificed her life to be present at this ball by her imprudence in concealing from her mother the symptoms of the distemper. The Prince Imperial was seriously ill, and was nursed night and day by the Empress herself, with very natural anxiety and the greatest maternal devotion. In all probability, had she been able to have her own way, her child would have been subjected to far stricter discipline, and certainly more judicious management. But the Emperor could not be induced to resist the child's wishes in anything he fancied. In the ordinary evenings at the Tuileries the little Prince and his playfellows romped and rushed about without restraint, leaping over the ottomans, and pursuing each other with deafening noise. The Emperor particularly liked quiet; but he never allowed his son to be restrained, or went beyond a remark, in a tone of gentle resignation, as to "what a noise" they were making. Of course no one else could object. Often, when the Emperor was conversing seriously, the little Prince would put in his word and give his opinion. The Empress judiciously reprimanded him; but the Emperor stopped her immediately: "No, no; I like to hear him say what he thinks. So that is your opinion, Loulou?"

Fortunately for the little Prince, the policy which required that his education should have a military stamp, caused him to be put under the supreme command of General Frossard, who was appointed "Governor to the Prince Imperial," and who treated him according to military discipline without allowing any one to interfere.

The Emperor was wise enough to feel the necessity for this firmness, and was not sorry to hand over to another the control which might make his son "love him" less. His over-tender feelings were, however, often tried severely. The young Prince was heard to say on some festive occasion: "I should *so* like to stay! *He* won't let me." The Emperor, with his usual indulgence, answered: "Give me your cap; I will put it in my pocket—you can't go without it, and that will cause some delay." The little Prince then said ruefully: "It is of no use. I have tried that before! He has got another one ready!" And the terrible "he," General

Frossard, marched off his imperial charge under the care of his tutor.

The General maintained his authority against the Emperor himself unflinchingly. When the latter sent for the little Prince, during his studies, to show him to some political personage, General Frossard did not hesitate to "respectfully inform His Majesty that the Prince's studies would not be interrupted before another half hour." The Emperor would then smile and acquiesce.

CHAPTER XIV

The military element in Parisian society — Pélissier and Canrobert — Anecdotes of the former — How he treated a coward — A defective omelet and its consequences — His uncivilized manners — His marriage — The Duchesse de Malakoff — Canrobert — His marriage — Madame Canrobert — Pretensions of the marshal checked by the Emperor — An apparently ill-assorted but happy pair — Honorable character of Canrobert — MacMahon — Castellane — Magnan — Bosquet — Characteristic anecdote of the Emperor — Vaillant — Randon — Three inappropriate Christian names — Bazaine.

THE military element has always a great influence in Parisian society. Among the "heroes" who attracted the most attention at the court, the most prominent were Pélissier and Canrobert, both marshals of France, both having had supreme command in the Crimea, and each one having his own zealous partizans. Those of Pélissier extolled his energy and military spirit, criticizing the slowness and indecision of Canrobert, while the admirers of the latter dwelt on the inhumanity of Pélissier, and his reckless sacrifice of human life to reach his ends, attributing the indecision of Canrobert to his repugnance to unnecessary bloodshed, as his personal bravery could not be questioned.

There were ugly stories of the proceedings of

Pélissier; for instance, when he was in Algeria, it was charged that he suffocated with smoke the Arabs who had taken refuge in caves, where they all perished.[1] This barbarous mode of warfare caused an outburst of indignation in France at the time.

All acknowledged that Canrobert had behaved very nobly, and in a true soldierly spirit, when he was called upon to resign his command in the Crimea into the hands of Pélissier, without, on that occasion, showing a thought of selfishness, or the least hesitation in his military obedience. Although the pitiless brutality of Pélissier could not be denied, it was allowed that his determined energy brought him success in what he undertook, and gave him great influence over his men.

In an engagement with the Arabs in Algeria, an unfortunate officer holding the rank of captain was seized by panic, turned his horse, and fled to the village where the troops were stationed.

Of course a court-martial was appointed to judge the case, which met with severe punishment; but, in the interval, Pélissier, who was then colonel, met the culprit (who had pleaded sudden illness) in the street, and stood before him, sternly eying him from head to foot in silence.

At last the unfortunate man asked: "Do you want anything from me, colonel?"

In withering tones, with a marked emphasis on every word, Pélissier answered:

[1] In 1845 at Ouled-Rhéa.

DUC DE MALAKOFF.
FROM A PHOTOGRAPH BY BRAUN CLÉMENT & CO.

DUCHESSE DE MALAKOFF.
FROM A PHOTOGRAPH BY LA JEUNESSE.

"Yes! I want to see the face of *a coward*. For I have never yet met with one in the French army."

Violent as he was, he yet possessed the faculty of recognizing his fault, when he had gone too far. On one occasion, in some large town, he went to a restaurant for his luncheon. Pélissier liked good fare, when he could get it, and ordered an omelet with truffles. The waiter, against all rule, brought the omelet and the condiment on separate dishes.

Pélissier flew into a towering rage, abused the waiter, and finally threw the contents of the two dishes in his face. The waiter happened to have been a soldier, and had served in the Zouaves. He flew at Pélissier, who then had a narrow escape of his life, and returned home in woful condition. When he had recovered from the effects of his chastisement, he returned to the same restaurant, and ordered the same dish of the same waiter. The man brought it this time in proper condition. Pélissier then said to him:

"Well, I see that you are a brave fellow, who won't be bullied; take this," and he handed him twenty francs, which must have surprised him considerably.

When the marriage of this coarse, rough soldier of fortune[1] was officially announced, every one was

---

[1] Pélissier was born in 1794, of a family belonging to the peasant class, but in comparatively comfortable circumstances. He was educated first at the military preparatory school of La Flèche, and then went to St. Cyr.

astonished, for the bride was a young and beautiful Spaniard, Mademoiselle Sofia Valera della Pañega, a distant relative of the Empress Eugénie, under whose patronage this ill-assorted union had been arranged.

The Empress Eugénie was fond of match-making; but she was not usually fortunate in the results of those which she suggested, for her impetuous nature did not allow her to examine both sides of a question, or to weigh objections. In this case Mademoiselle della Pañega was a poor relative, who lived with the Comtesse de Montijo as a *protégée*. By marrying Pélissier, she would be a "maréchale" and Duchesse de Malakoff; what could be better? As to the life which she would lead when married to a man so much older than herself, whose ways and manners were those of a common soldier, with a violent temper besides, no one stopped to consider. And so poor Mademoiselle della Pañega, gentle, submissive, and fearing to offend, became the wife of Pélissier, who was old enough to have been her father instead of her husband. She complained to no one, and always behaved with great propriety and dignity; but her face was sufficiently eloquent. A few years after her marriage she became a widow.[1]

The characteristic behavior of Pélissier, notably on the very day of his wedding, as he left the

---

[1] In 1864. Pélissier was then Governor-General of Algeria. He had married Mademoiselle della Pañega in 1858, at the age of sixty-four.

church, cannot be dwelt upon in these pages, nor other traits depicting his oddities in general society.

One instance, however, I may mention, which, though trifling, may give some idea of his uncivilized ways and manners. The Comtesse B—— related in my presence that while on a visit to her sister, the Duchess of Manchester, where Pélissier, who was then ambassador in England, was among the guests, she met him one morning as she was going down-stairs.

"Stop, Comtesse," said Pélissier, "you have a black mark on your forehead."

Then, wetting his finger in his mouth, he obligingly rubbed the place and removed the stain.

Canrobert[1] was, at that time, a short square-built man, with a large head out of proportion to his figure, and proverbially ill-favored and ungainly; but, though rather predisposed to gasconading and flourish, he was of a totally different stamp and education from Pélissier. He married a very pretty and distinguished Scotch lady—a Miss Macdonald (of the great Scotch clan so named), whom he absolutely worshiped, and who was devoted to him, ill-assorted as they seemed to be. They were known in society as "Caliban and Ariel"; but they were a most united couple and very happy together. The poor old Marshal was perfectly heart-broken when his wife was taken from him

[1] Certain Canrobert, or de Canrobert, was born in 1809, and was the son of an officer of good family in the *emigré* army. He died in Paris, February, 1895.

in the year 1890. As she was lowered into her grave, the veteran wept like a child, exclaiming in a voice broken by sobs: "'T is I, 't is I who should lie there!"

He reached a great age, universally respected as a most honorable and excellent man, apart from his remarkable military talents and heroic personal valor.

Madame Canrobert was as intelligent as she was elegant and refined; she had a perfect appreciation of the duties which her high position involved, and, during the disastrous war, as during the Empire, she performed them admirably. When she was first married, the marshal held the important command of the army corps at Lyons, and his exaggerated view of what was due to her as his wife caused, at first, some ill feeling among the military aristocracy and their wives, and offended the civil authorities considerably.

It was said that when Canrobert gave his first official dinner, the Prefect, as the highest functionary present, stepped forward to offer his arm to Madame Canrobert, as a matter of course; but the Marshal interposed, saying that he alone could take in La Maréchale. This mortification to the Prefect caused considerable animadversion, but when Canrobert ordered that La Maréchale should never go out in her carriage without being attended by a military escort, there was a general outcry, as the Empress herself did not have one habitually. Matters reached such a seething condition that the Emperor was obliged to interfere, so that the limits of Madame Canrobert's privileges might be clearly defined.

But this was only a passing cloud, due to inexperience.

MacMahon had not attracted much notice before the Italian war, although his noble conduct at the taking of the Malakoff tower at Sebastopol deserved more fame. He was loaded with honors after Magenta, but he was not much seen in the society of the court, as he belonged to the Faubourg St. Germain by his own family ties, and especially those of his wife, a daughter of the Duc de Castries. MacMahon was in all things strictly honorable and faithful to his duty toward the Emperor, but he did not seek to do more, and made no demonstrations.

The other marshals were only remarkable for their military achievements, except Castellane, a distinguished man in every respect, noted for his energy, his determination, and his high military spirit, who commanded at Lyons in almost vice-regal fashion. His daughter, who was extremely popular, married the Minister of Prussia, Count Hatzfeldt, and, after his death, the Duc de Valençay, of the Talleyrand-Périgord family.

Magnan had helped in the "coup d'état," and was, consequently, much favored by the Emperor; but there was a strong feeling against him, because he was the Grand Master of the Freemasons in France, and was, consequently, antagonistic to the clergy.

Bosquet had greatly distinguished himself in the Crimea, and especially at Inkerman, where his timely arrival saved the English allies, who were nearly overpowered. He was an ardent Republican, and, consequently, opposed to the Empire and the Emperor. At the time of the "coup d'état" he asked to be released from active service; his demand was refused, though his feelings were shown so plainly that he gave up all hope of high promotion. But in yielding to such supposition he did not appreciate the justice and generosity of the Emperor, who recognized his merits and loaded him with honors. After the Crimea the army had declared that he deserved the highest of all distinctions, the "bâton" of a marshal of France, but Bosquet was convinced that his opinions and his friendships with the Emperor's most marked adversaries would prevent him from ever reaching that supreme honor. To his surprise, after the peace, he was invited to dine at the Tuileries. He went, as in duty bound; the dinner passed without any particular incident, but when the dessert had been placed upon the table, the Emperor, addressing his guests, said:

"Gentlemen, fill your glasses. I wish to propose a toast — the health of two of my friends here present. To Marshal Canrobert! To Marshal Bosquet!"

Both remained speechless, overcome with joy and gratitude, but when Bosquet took the hand which the Emperor frankly extended to him, his heart was won, and he became devoted to the Emperor from that hour. Unfortunately, he died at a comparatively early age.

Vaillant was a man of humble origin—betrayed by his manners. He boasted of being the son of a cobbler. Such a rise in life is certainly very honorable, but it was unnecessary to prove the fact so continually and so evidently. He was at the head of the household, which he governed officially, and had apartments in the palace next to those of the Comte de Tascher. He was a very ordinary-looking man, and enormously stout.

Randon was considered very estimable in private life, but he played only a secondary part. He was looked upon as rather too prudent in military tactics. There were many jests on the inappropriate Christian names of the three marshals Canrobert, Randon, and Pélissier.

The prudent Randon's given name was "Cæsar"; Canrobert, noted for his indecision, was called "Certain"; and Pélissier, whose roughness was proverbial, had been christened "Amable."

Bazaine was then in Mexico, and had not yet reached the rank of marshal; his reputation on his return was not of a kind to entitle him to such a recompense! The failure of the campaign and the disastrous fate of Maximilian were openly attributed to his incapacity, if not treachery, which foreshadowed his conduct during the Franco-German war.

CHAPTER XV.

Monsieur Thouvenel — A French ambassador at Constantinople — A night spent in Oriental luxury — Its questionable delights — A parrot's reprimand to an ambassador — Monsieur Thouvenel, Minister of Foreign Affairs — Policy of Monsieur Thouvenel — Opposition of the Emperor and Empress — The Emperor's speech on opening the Legislative Assembly — Feeling of the nation — Thouvenel obliged to resign — The child and the Emperor — Generosity of the latter — Petition of a Legitimist lady — Plain speaking — Chivalrous conduct of the Emperor — His noble nature.

MONSIEUR THOUVENEL, who was Minister for Foreign Affairs after the Italian war, was an old and intimate friend of the de Tascher family. I well remember his intense pride and delight when the great question of the annexation of Savoy and Nice was finally settled, and he had the satisfaction, which he desired beyond any other, of signing his name to the treaty which gave both to France.

"If I can only write Thouvenel below that treaty, I shall die happy!" he exclaimed in my presence.

When I first saw M. Thouvenel he was ambassador at Constantinople, and being in Paris on a diplomatic *congé*, he came to dine at the Tuileries with the de Taschers. He had much to relate, for which we were in some degree prepared by the graphic account

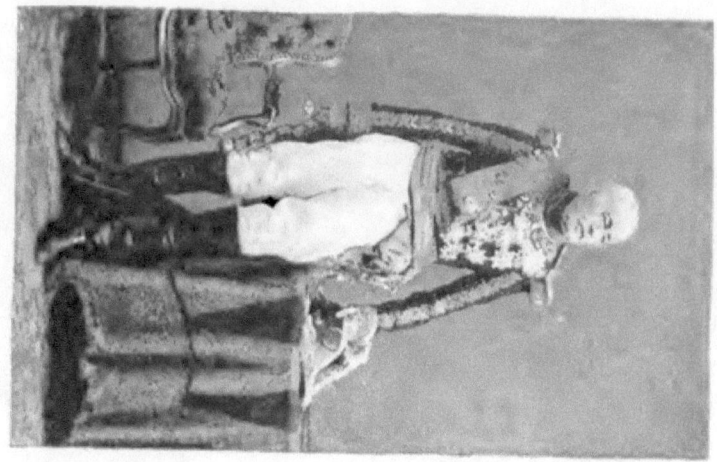

MARSHAL CASTELLANE.
FROM A PHOTOGRAPH BY LADREY-DISDERI.

MARSHAL RANDON.
FROM A PHOTOGRAPH BY LADREY-DISDERI.

of a mutual friend, who had described a visit of M. Thouvenel to some Aga or Pasha; where, after having dined principally on a variety of luscious sweetmeats, he was obliged to spend the night in a magnificent apartment, lighted brilliantly by an immense chandelier, with negro slaves lying before his door to guard his person, and snoring so loudly that sleep was impossible; while his rest was still further disturbed by the discomfort of his splendid bed, where white satin sheets exasperated his nerves and set his teeth on edge, and a pillow covered with cloth of gold scratched his face and tore his hair.

My young charges had particularly enjoyed this picture of Oriental luxury, so that the presence of M. Thouvenel, with his animated conversation, and all he had to relate, was extremely welcome. He was a tall, powerful man, with rather a pompous demeanor, but a great talker, and, as he unbent with the de Taschers more than usual, he was really very agreeable. Every one was listening with great interest to his graphic descriptions, when, to his own astonishment, and the intense amusement of the younger members of the family, his eloquence was suddenly cut short by the energetic protestations of a favorite parrot, who, being disturbed in his slumbers, vociferated, "Tais-toi, Édouard!"

The Christian name of the narrator being Édouard, the remark was decidedly personal, and no one could help laughing, while M. Thouvenel, utterly amazed, declared: "Why, he is actually attacking *me!*"

11

The parrot had been brought from Pernambuco by a Spanish priest, as a present to the Empress Eugénie, and had been taught pretty speeches in her honor. The Empress, having no fondness for parrots, gave this one — a particularly fine specimen — to the Duc de Tascher. But the family being absent from home, the Duke did not know what to do with it, and put it to board with an old woman at St. Cloud, who took great care of the bird, but established it on her window-sill, where the street gamins held conversations with her charge, by no means to the improvement of its vocabulary. When the family returned to the Tuileries the parrot had learned French, but swore in most disreputable fashion, and held such language that he was not considered fit to be introduced into society. Gradually, however, new words blotted out the old ones, and the Duke's daughters then delighted in teaching him sentences, which he picked up with the greatest facility. Every morning, he began the day with energetic protestations of "Vive l' Empereur!" at the same time commanding military drill, in sonorous, officer-like tones, which were indescribably ludicrous. He was a great favorite in the family, but after his attack on M. Thouvenel was banished from the drawing-room in the evening.

We tried on one occasion to show off his talents to the Empress Eugénie, who had said eagerly: "Oh, do make him talk!" But he was obstinately silent. "Just like children," as she said, laughing.

When Monsieur Thouvenel became Minister of

Foreign Affairs after the Italian war, he took the anti-papal side so warmly that the family de Tascher no longer approved of him, for they were sincere Catholics, and consequently averse to the spoliation of the Pope, which at that time the Emperor sincerely wished to avoid, while the Empress, with her usual ardor, strongly opposed it. This was the origin of the so-called " clerical" views attributed to the Empress, which, in fact, were limited to this sole point.

The nation at that time, or at least its representatives in the Chamber of Deputies and the Senate, strongly favored the policy of supporting the Pope and his temporal power, as I was able to judge from the manner in which the Emperor's speech was received at the opening of the Corps Législatif.

I was in a gallery exactly opposite the throne, in the " Salle des États " of the Louvre, where the Emperor received the two Houses; a magnificent hall, where the Senators in uniform and the Corps Législatif were already seated, waiting for the Emperor, whose throne, raised on steps, was before them. An inclosed space was reserved for the Empress and her suite below the throne on the Emperor's right hand, but at the side, and not facing the assembly.

The Empress, holding the Prince Imperial by the hand, passed through the gallery, where I stood with other privileged spectators, and stopped with a sort of graceful diffidence to give a general bow to all present. Her refined and delicate beauty seemed more exquisite than ever on that occasion, in her picturesque dress and mantle of white satin, bordered with the dark fur of the Russian sable, and falling round her in rich soft folds as she moved with her usual grace.

The little Prince wore his habitual suit of black velvet, with red stockings; his pretty brown curls resting on his large collar of rich lace.

When he had taken his seat by the side of his mother, "L'Empereur!" was announced in a loud voice, and the Emperor, in the full uniform of a general, with his broad red ribbon of the Legion of Honor, ascended the steps of the throne and took his seat.

All had risen on his entrance, but resumed their seats to hear the speech.

He began in a loud, clear voice, every word distinctly audible:

"Messieurs les Sénateurs! Messieurs les Députés!"

Every one listened in dead silence, but there was an occasional wave in the crowd when any sentence was of particular interest.

At last he raised his voice: "With regard to matters concerning Italy —"

There was an immense surging motion in the Assembly, with exclamations— "Ah! ah!" while all leaned forward eagerly, seeming to drink in his words.

The Emperor had paused till silence was completely restored; then he continued, distinctly stating his wishes and intentions: finally, raising his voice, he added with marked emphasis: "Without forsaking the Holy Father, whom our rights and our duty oblige us to support."

There was another great wave; again there were exclamations of "Ah! ah!" but in tones of joyful relief, followed by a pealing shout, like the roll of thunder, "Vive l' Empereur!" repeated three times.

The effect was electrifying. There could be no doubt that all France was with him then.

Monsieur Thouvenel, however, persisted in his views, going so far beyond the Emperor and displeasing the Empress to such a degree, that he was finally obliged to send in his resignation, which, as he was an ambitious man, cost him great bitterness of spirit.

Shortly afterward, the Emperor, one morning, was walking in the Bois de Boulogne, with his aide-de-camp (*officier d'ordonnance*), when a young child ran his hoop against him. The Emperor caught the hoop, and gave it back to the child, at the same time, with his usual kindness, stooping to kiss him. The boy pushed him away roughly, and the aide-de-camp exclaimed: "But the Emperor wishes to kiss you! You must kiss the Emperor!"

"No," cried the child, "I won't kiss him! He is a very bad man! My papa says so, and he hates him!"

"What is your father's business?" asked the Emperor quietly.

"Business! My papa has no business! He does nothing at all — *he is a senator!*"

The senators being especially appointed by the Emperor himself amongst those supposed to be most faithful to him, the revelation was startling. The aide-de-camp indignantly inquired:

"What is your father's name?"

The Emperor laid his hand on his arm.

"Hush! *la recherche de la paternité est interdite.*"

And he turned away without hearing the name so nearly betrayed.

But the story was repeated, and curiosity was awakened, the age of the child causing suspicion to point strongly toward Thouvenel, the senators being mostly old men; but the fact was never positively elucidated.

The generosity shown by the Emperor on this occasion was highly characteristic. I remember an instance of a different kind, which came to my personal knowledge. A lady who was a friend of some of my cousins, having a favor to solicit, obtained a private audience of the Emperor. She was shown into his private cabinet, where he received her with the cold, calm courtesy which marked his habitual manner. She began—with what seemed great boldness, and was, in reality, excellent diplomacy—by telling him that although she came to proffer a petition, she must first make a confession; that all the members of her family were his political adversaries, being zealous Legitimists, and devoted to that cause. The Emperor listened calmly in silence. She then explained the favor that she had come to ask, and pleaded her cause. Still the Emperor listened with grave attention, asking a few questions, but without giving any indication of his feelings or of his decision.

When she had finished her statement, and stopped speaking, she looked anxiously toward him; but he simply made the usual motion indicating that she might retire. She moved toward the door, courteously followed by the Emperor; and then, suddenly turning to him, she said:

"Sire! may I take some hope with me?"

"Take certainty, madame," answered the Emperor, with that peculiarly charming smile which at rare intervals lighted up his grave face.

The appeal to the noble side of his nature was never made in vain.

In general, it was said that when a favor was asked, and the Emperor listened in silence, twirling his mustache, the petition might be looked upon as granted; but when he stroked his chin downward, and said seriously, "*C'est bien difficile*" (It is a difficult matter), then it was a case where hope must be given up.

Such were the variations of the court barometer, which all watched carefully.

CHAPTER XVI

Clouds in the sky of the Empire — The Mexican War unpopular — "L'Empire, c'est la paix!" — Financial difficulties — Extravagant tendencies of the Emperor — The yacht built for the Empress — The Hôtel d'Albe built and destroyed — Expenses of Compiègne and Fontainebleau — Costly artistic mistakes — The Emperor's lavish generosity — Too many improvements in Paris — Spanish preferences of the Empress — She goes to bull fights — The Empress goes to Spain — Death of the Duc de Morny.

MY younger pupil, Hortense de Tascher was now gradually introduced into society, and finally, at the age of eighteen, she was admitted to the court balls, and invited to the festivities of Compiègne and Fontainebleau — expensive and fatiguing pleasures, more dreaded than welcomed by those honored with invitations.

There were clouds in the sky of the Empire, which had been noticed even before the time to which I now allude. The war in Mexico was extremely unpopular; no one understood why French money and French blood should be sacrificed to place an Austrian archduke on a throne in another hemisphere. The Italian war had been unwillingly accepted, but it had been successful, and France had gained Nice and Savoy. Glory and increase of territory will always be received in France as an adequate compensation for many sacrifices; but the Emperor had said: "L'Empire c'est la paix" and the Italian war had been preceded by that of the Crimea, and was closely followed by the war in Mexico, for which no motive could be found beyond an imaginative fancy of the Empress, worked upon by Mexican adventurers who had gained her ear. The immense responsibility, so easily assumed, was new and most displeasing to the French, who, imbued with the principle of the Salic law, have no wish to be governed by women. Even in the case of regencies,—and the two examples of Marie de Médicis and Anne of Austria had left unfavorable impressions — the real rulers were undoubtedly Richelieu and Mazarin. The only instance of a Queen-Consort interfering directly and persistently in public affairs was the very unfortunate case of Marie Antoinette. Enormous sums were spent for Mexico; and at the same time it was well known that the national finances were in a bad state. Improvements, especially in Paris, had been carried on too fast and at too great a cost. The Emperor seemed to have no idea of the value of money, either with regard to the funds of the nation or his own private expenses. Generous, even to extravagance, he gave to all who asked; and not only to promote scientific inventions or to encourage charitable institutions, which might have been approved, but also to those who appealed to him for their private interests, and not always honorable debts. There was no gambling in the Emperor's private circle; but some of the courtiers gambled elsewhere, and lost large sums at play. The Emperor's assistance was then implored, with threats of suicide and public scandal. Others became involved in speculations, the fever of the period. These were sometimes of a doubtful kind. Matters were then hushed up, and the Emperor paid. There were other important sums spent for other expenses,— to which we can only allude,— the least justifiable of all. The Emperor had a very large Civil List from the nation; but he was obliged to keep up all the imperial palaces, with their furniture, gardens, and repairs at his own expense. The court was established on a splendid scale; its functionaries were only too numerous, and they were all well paid. In the beginning of the Empire, money had seemed inexhaustible, and had been largely squandered in empty, and often unnecessary magnificence. Both the Emperor and Empress seemed to imagine that they had in their possession the purse of fairy tales, which is always full of gold. The Empress, soon after her marriage, had a fancy for a yacht of her own. Immediately a beautiful little toy was built for her, too small to be of any use, but a little gem, with the greatest luxury shown in every detail. She had the beautiful Hôtel d'Albe[1] built for her

---

[1] The ball previously described took place in this residence.

sister, and no expense was spared to make it perfect. The Duchess of Alva died there shortly after the splendid ball which had been given for its inauguration. The Empress then could no longer endure to see it, and it was recklessly pulled down, after only a few months of use. How unreasonable this act was, under the circumstances, will be easily understood; it was much regretted by all around her.[1]

The expenses of Compiègne and Fontainebleau were enormous, out of all proportion to any advantage to be gained by such lavish hospitality; and these were continued yearly.

The Emperor was easily talked over by those who, like Viollet-le-Duc, the well-known architect, appealed to him in the name of "art"—a subject strangely foreign to his natural faculties. The Emperor was a remarkable mathematician, and was also strongly attracted by scientific pursuits; but "art" was an unknown language to him. The Empress had some pretensions to a better understanding of the subject; but according to the judgment of real connoisseurs her taste was far from pure, and she was attracted more by showy appearances than by real artistic merit. The whole style of the Empire was too ornate and meretricious.

The worst consequence of these various influ-

[1] The Avenue de l'Alma was opened on the spot previously occupied by the "Hôtel d'Albe." An hotel for travelers, near the place, took the name, but has nothing in common with the destroyed residence.

ences, was that of leading the Emperor to spend enormous sums in undertakings of a doubtful advantage, by no means universally approved in the artistic world, and, at all events, wholly unnecessary.

General Rolin, the Comptroller of the Household, was a scrupulously honest man, who looked conscientiously into the smallest details, and who, while keeping up the splendor and liberality which characterized the living arrangements of the Imperial residences, yet watchfully stopped abuses, and managed so judiciously that he often kept within the sum allowed him, so as to have a surplus, which he carefully handed to the Treasurer. But all were not so able, nor perhaps so scrupulous, and the careless generosity of the Emperor was preyed upon; the result of this universal openhandedness being that, after he had reigned eighteen years with enormous sums at his disposal, the personal property of Napoleon III. at the time of his death was sworn under £120,000 in the Probate Court of London.

The Empress was more prudent than the Emperor in her private expenses, but her allowance was very large, and her fancies, as we have seen, were not always reasonable.

The Empress was unpopular, a great deal that was blamed being attributed to her influence, the supposed effects of which irritated the general feeling, that she was not in her rightful place.

Unfortunately, according to the testimony of many who were so situated as to be able to judge her actions, she never understood the requirements of her high position as the wife of the sovereign ruler of France. She was a Spanish lady of high degree, and such she remained, without ever bringing to her mind the truth contained in the French proverb *Qui prend mari prend patrie* (Who takes a husband takes a fatherland). In the final catastrophe during the war, she very nobly asserted the interests of France, with the sacrifice of those concerning the throne and the dynasty; had she always acted in the same spirit, she would have gained the good-will of the nation; but, unfortunately, she never, till then, showed French preferences. She had an English nurse for her son; an excellent choice, but not judicious with regard to the feeling of the nation. Because the Queen of England dressed her children in Highland garb, she had a Highland costume made for the Prince Imperial, without understanding that what was perfectly suitable for the descendants of the kings of Scotland, became a mere masquerade for the son of the Bonapartes. These are trifles, it may be objected; but such trifles, of frequent occurrence, have a greater influence on the public mind than she imagined; for she always acted like a private individual whose fancies pass unnoticed. In the south of France, when she went to Biarritz, she attended bull-fights, wearing her Spanish mantilla, with a pomegranate flower in her hair, following all the incidents of the horrid scene with the greatest excitement, clapping her hands and uttering loud Spanish cries of encouragement, according to the custom of Madrid, but which seemed strangely misplaced in the case of a French Empress.

On one of these occasions she had gone with her suite to see the bulls in their inclosure, the day before the *corrida*, and as she drew very near to the fence, she was cautioned as to possible danger.

"Oh, no," she replied, "they are Spanish bulls, and I have nothing to fear from them."

As she spoke, a low suppressed bellow was heard just behind her. Although they were "Spanish bulls," her confidence in their sagacity did not seem complete, for she uttered a loud scream and took flight with great rapidity, till the laughter she heard caused her to look back, when she recognized that she had an adversary near her no more dangerous than the Duc de Tascher, who had mischievously put her nerves to the test.

When she was at Biarritz the Empress tried to look as Spanish as she could, and wore fanciful dresses with as much bright scarlet as possible. The Prince de Chimay told me that one day, seeing a group of ladies very brilliantly attired, with a great deal of red about them, he had supposed that they were the wives of the "toreros," or champions of the bull-fight, but, on drawing near to examine them, he was thunderstruck as he recognized the Empress and her ladies.

The Empress had a great wish to return to Spain and to show herself in her present dignity. There were strong objections to this, and Mérimée,[1] who, as an old and intimate friend of the Comtesse de Montijo, had some influence over her daughter, tried in vain to point out to her the difficulties which would arise, the false position in which she would be placed. He relates amusingly in his letters the discussion with the Empress Eugénie, who persisted in asserting that she did not see why she could not go to Spain, if she chose, like other people. Mérimée answered: "Because queens and empresses cannot do what other people do; they are subjected to a number of impediments which do not concern other people; this is the case with all sovereigns — and this is the reason why I have always refused all the crowns which have been offered to me." The conclusion, uttered with absolute gravity of tone, first caused the Empress to open her eyes wide; then she laughed heartily, but still would not yield. Soon afterward she began to cruise round the coast of Spain, landing at Gibraltar, Valencia, Cadiz, etc., so as to provoke an invitation to Madrid from Queen Isabella, which was duly sent. The Empress was not likely to lose such an opportunity, and though with an insufficient suite, she immediately went to Madrid, where the Queen received her at the royal palace.

The obeisance of a subject to the sovereign, according to Spanish etiquette, requires that the knee should almost touch the ground. This was most gracefully performed by the Empress, but, although

[1] The well-known French writer.

perfect for Mademoiselle de Montijo, was it quite appropriate as an homage from the wife of the Emperor of the French?

The Queen of Spain was naturally much gratified, but the French suite had dubious feelings on the subject, which was much talked of on their return. The Spaniards received her very coldly, and made no demonstrations, but the Queen honored her visit with the usual receptions, a ball, a state visit to the opera, and last, not least, a bull-fight.

The Empress returned, delighted with her visit. But the French were still more inclined to repeat what had been said before: "She was determined to become an Empress. Well, now, let her act like one!" Even her deference to the Queen of England was deemed excessive by French pride.

And yet her simplicity, and the almost pleading diffidence of her manner on official occasions, had a great charm, and were certainly more creditable to her than the haughtiness which so many would have mistaken for dignity in such a change of position.

It must be admitted, however, that the Empress, at times, weary of the restraints of her rank, threw them off too recklessly. When she went to England and Scotland for a change of scene after the death of her sister, the Duchess of Alva, she attracted very unfavorable notice in London, where, at that time especially, ladies of rank were subjected to strict rules of custom and decorum.

DUCHESS OF ALVA AND CHILDREN.

Lord Malmesbury says, in his "Memoirs of an ex-Minister":

"The Empress of the French arrived in London, and drove with her suite to Claridge's Hotel in hack cabs. The following morning she went out shopping, on foot, and to the Crystal Palace in the afternoon."

I well remember the surprise and displeasure of all the English who spoke to me on the subject at the time. These small incidents confirmed the general impression that royalty is a trade which must be learned like any other.

The death of the Duc de Morny, which occurred just at the time when difficulties were beginning to gather round the Emperor, was deeply felt by him; the more deeply that the blow was very sudden. Morny had been in weak health for some time, but no one dreamed of any danger. His constitution was, however, really giving way, and an accidental chill, producing a sort of diphtheria, ended his life with fearful rapidity.

The Emperor and Empress both attended his sick bed; the former was deeply affected. The loss to him was indeed irreparable. Morny's interests and his own were identical. Morny was naturally devoted to the Empire, while his clear intellect, his determined spirit, and his far more practical views, were of immense assistance to the Emperor, who was too imaginative, and often too sentimental. The question of "sensibility" never stood in the way of Morny's intentions or plans. He had a considerable amount of acute good sense, very little heart, and no principle; but he possessed charming and captivating manners, with the appearance of having all that was really deficient; withal he had perfect self-command and considerable personal courage, always seeing clearly before him the wished-for goal, and going straight to it without looking to the right or left.

No one could conciliate adversaries so well as Morny; he always knew what to say, and how to say it, without being stopped by inconvenient scruples or too rigid principles.

Had Morny lived, many mistakes might have been avoided when the time of trial came; his irresistible influence would certainly have been felt, and might have prevented the evils which led to the downfall of the unhappy Emperor, who was fated to lose his best advisers at the time when their presence was most needed.

But Morny died; there was a magnificent funeral; his wife gave way to the most violent grief; he was the subject of all conversations for some time, with praise and blame, both of which were deserved, and then, as usual, he was forgotten. His official place was taken, though not filled — and his wife finally married a Spanish grandee, the Duc de Sesto.

Such is the world. The more serious among his numerous friends found some comfort in the fact that the Archbishop of Paris had spent considerable time by his bedside to prepare him for the last hour, and had administered the rites of the Catholic Church to the dying man, who, though certainly faulty, was not impenitent. He left four young children; the eldest, then only seven years old, is now Duc de Morny.

CHAPTER XVII

Evenings in the apartments of the Duchesse de Tascher—Madame Ristori, the tragic actress — How a stage queen ate asparagus — Her conversation — Sixteen thousand pounds of luggage — Danger in a glass of lemonade — Recitations — The real dress of Queen Mary on the scaffold — Madame Ristori's impersonation of Mary Stuart — The evil eye — The value of stage bouquets as a mark of public enthusiasm — Leopold von Mayer — How he played the piano with his fists — He plays before the Sultan — Death of the Archbishop of Bourges — The Papal Nuncio — Prince Chigi — Djemil Pasha, the Turkish Ambassador — Marriage of Hortense de Tascher to the Comte de l'Espine.

AMONG the remarkable visitors received in the evenings by the Duchesse de Tascher was the tragic actress Madame Ristori, who had married the Marchese Capranica del Grillo, and was treated as a "marquise" although she had not given up the stage. I felt a great curiosity to see her in private life, and was delighted when I first heard that she was coming to dinner like any ordinary mortal. She was rather late, which disturbed the punctual habits of the family, but just as some annoyance was felt and expressed she appeared, followed by her small, insignificant husband—a gentleman, evidently, but not remarkable in any respect. Madame

Ristori struck me as a very handsome woman, tall and majestic in appearance, very natural and good-humored, without any stage affectation, but not to be mistaken for a gentlewoman, however well she might play queens. Her whole figure and her motions recalled the Italian *Contadina* or peasant-woman; not the high-born *Signora*. She talked a great deal, with animated gestures and a full, mellow contralto voice, which every now and then went off into a stage intonation, but was usually agreeable, though she threw into everything she said a degree of fire and excitement not usual in general society.

I was particularly amused by the peculiar way in which the tragic queen disposed of the asparagus on her plate. The tips were first daintily cut off; but then a knife held as firmly as her stage dagger gathered them up, while her thumb secured them on the point and thus conveyed them to her lips with great and rapid dexterity.

She constantly appealed to her husband as "Giuliano." He seemed utterly weary of his task of leading "Madame," as he called his wife, all over the world, with her theatrical satellites and her enormous amount of luggage, on which she inquired for our information:

"Giuliano! Quanto peso abbiamo noi?"[1]

He answered, "Sixteen thousand pounds"; which may truly be considered as an incumbrance.

He told me, as an example of the equivocal de-

---

[1] "What weight do we take with us?"

lights of the position, that "Madame" had been once poisoned by a rival actress. When she came off the stage in a state of dramatic fever, Madame was in the habit of drinking eagerly a large glass of lemonade. On this occasion her amiable rival had steeped a bundle of lucifer matches in the lemonade, which naturally produced extremely unpleasant consequences, enabling "Madame" fully to understand the effects of poison in her tragic scenes; but, in this instance, fortunately stopping half-way, thanks to prompt medical assistance.

After dinner, she interested every one present by analyzing with great intelligence the character of Mary Stuart, one of her best impersonations. She told us that she had suppressed the love scenes with "Mortimer" in the tragedy, as unnatural under the circumstances.

"At the time of her death Queen Mary was forty-five; she had been a prisoner for eighteen years. Is it possible that she should then think of coquetting? No, no; my instinct (*mon instinct*) tells me that Mary Stuart's thoughts were all in heaven."

She related to us her opportunities of seeing historical relics of the time; the real veil of Queen Mary, and her real rosary, which she herself had been obliged to have otherwise for stage effect. The real veil is in white silk, of a texture which would now be considered coarse, with cross-barred lines of gold thread. The beads of the rosary are of dark-blue enamel, like lapis lazuli, and would not be effective on the black dress.

During this conversation the rooms had filled, and the Duchesse de Tascher then asked the interesting guest to recite some passages from "Maria Stuarda"; to which she acceded, very kindly and naturally, without pretension.

I must acknowledge that my first impression on seeing the visitor with whom I had just been conversing suddenly rush forward with clasped hands, and tragic exclamations, was that of a fit of insanity; but after a few words all was forgotten in the charm of that exquisite enunciation, and the melody of her voice, now swelling in tragic tones, now sinking to the softest murmur; while her face seemed transfigured. Every one was thrilled and captivated; but the surprise of the conclusion was as great as that of the beginning. When the last word had been uttered, with the most moving effect, she sat down and fanned herself as calmly as before, quite another individual, while all around her were too breathless to be able even to express their admiration at the first moment. Then she was surrounded and thanked, with entreaties for more, to which she yielded with great good nature, reciting both in French and Italian; but the former was much spoiled by the marked Italian accent, notwithstanding the merits of the interpretation.

Among the listeners was an Italian marchese, of the illustrious house of Visconti, and I expressed my admiration to him.

"Yes," he said, "she is a fine actress and a good

sort of woman; *ma una jettatrice*[1] ("but she has the evil eye").

"*Jettatrice!*" I exclaimed, in astonishment.

"Yes, *una jettatrice*. Look!" and he showed me his hand concealed under his coat; closed, with the forefinger and the little finger extended, like two horns, which is supposed to act as a countercharm.

"You see my hand. I shall not change that position of my fingers till she goes. Don't laugh,— I am quite in earnest, and it is quite necessary. Ask your Emperor whether she has the evil eye or not."

It was a curious coincidence that every time the Emperor had gone to see Madame Ristori perform some serious event had occurred, the last occasion being on the night of the Orsini explosions. But the tenacity with which the superstition of the evil eye is rooted in the minds of Italians is curious to observe.

Shortly afterward, I went with the Duchesse de Bassano to see Madame Ristori interpret the character of Queen Mary. I was fascinated, delighted, but was made miserable for some days afterward, which, a critic contended, should not be the effect of true art. The actress met with an enthusiastic reception, and a shower of bouquets fell at her feet when she was recalled after the heart-breaking execution of poor Mary — when the two blows of the axe had been heard by the audience. I mentioned the profusion

---

[1] A *jettatore*, or, in the feminine, *jettatrice*, is said of those who have "the evil eye," and are supposed to bring misfortune with them.

of flowers to Count Molin, a descendant of one of the Doges of Venice.

He answered very quietly: "Yes, I know. I threw them all."

"*You* threw them? You were so generous?"

"Not at all generous. I know La Ristori, and the flowers were brought to me in my box, with a request to throw them after the recall, following the great scene with Elizabeth. I threw them conscientiously as directed; they were brought back to me, and I threw them all again, according to orders, at the end of the play!"

This peep into stage trickery was amusing, but rather disconcerting as to the value of apparent enthusiasm!

Another almost regular visitor at the receptions of the Duchesse de Tascher was the celebrated pianist, now forgotten, Leopold von Mayer, whose tremendous execution was rather alarming for the safety of the instruments under his hands. He very often sent his own, which had been especially prepared for his performance, in which his closed fists actually played a part, to the amazement of the bystanders. How this was done was a puzzle difficult to solve. His favorite assertion, in his German-English, was: "My finkers are my slafes" (my fingers are my slaves); but fingers were not apparent in this instance. After comparing notes with the Duc de Bassano, we both came to the conclusion that the thumb, folded and protruding from under the closed fist, performed those strange wonders of unartistic jugglery.

There was a story of his having been summoned to play before the Sultan during a visit to Constantinople. Mayer was duly ushered into the august presence; but no instrument was visible, and he was wondering as to what was coming next, when he saw his piano appear, poised on the shoulders of four Turks, the usual supports having been unscrewed and removed. The indignation of the choleric German may be imagined, who insisted on the pristine condition being restored; but he was told that he must not sit down before the Sultan, and consequently being obliged to play standing, the instrument must be raised to his height. Mayer's fists would probably have floored the four Turks, and the piano with them, besides the inconvenience of such an unusual position; so, after an energetic battle, the Sultan yielded, and Mayer was able to perform in Christian fashion.

The kind and venerable Archbishop of Bourges died[1] about this time, and his loss was deeply felt by the whole family of de Tascher. I remember Hortense de Tascher bursting into tears at the luncheon-table, when his secretary was relating his last illness; how he spoke of the de Taschers and of his pleasant evenings with them, recalling the games of chess, and again saying with his characteristic simplicity: "I don't know how it is—I

[1] At his archiepiscopal palace of Bourges, not at the Tuileries.

really got the better of "Albion," but I never could conquer little Hortense."

Dear old man! There never was a better or purer soul—"even as that of a little child."

The Papal Nuncio, Prince Chigi, was a frequent visitor; a magnificent prelate in his purple robes; tall and of noble figure—his well-cut features of the most aristocratic type. He always left the rooms at ten o'clock, after taking tea, which I brought him myself as a mark of respect; when he would apologize again and again, with courteous politeness, repeating: "Troppo buona! troppo buona." (too kind.)

Djemil Pasha, the Turkish ambassador, was also a frequent guest. He was amusingly fond of tea, made in British fashion, and always came anxiously to inquire of me if I was to make it, or if it was left to the servants. If I replied that, the party being large, the servants undertook that care, he groaned:

"Oh! what a pity!"

I remained for two more years under these pleasant circumstances with my dear pupil, Hortense de Tascher de la Pagerie, to whom I was most deeply attached—one of the sweetest beings I have ever met in the whole course of my life, and whose untimely death, which so soon followed her happy marriage with the Comte de l'Espine, was mourned as a sort of public calamity by all who knew her, even if only by name.[1]

[1] Her daughter is now the Princess Louis de Croy.

CHAPTER XVIII

I leave the Tuileries — Opinion in the provinces — The Empress severely judged — Exaggerated reports — Intimacy with Metternich and Nigra — Why the Emperor disapproved — Opinion expressed by the Duc de Tascher on the Empress, before her marriage — Outbreak of the cholera — Her admirable conduct — How an Empress "stands fire" — Nature and education of the Empress Eugénie — The Empress Augusta of Germany — The Empress Eugénie visits charitable institutions — Mlle. Bouvet — The Empress visits the poor — Goes to Belleville and other dangerous places — Excellent intentions not always wisely carried out — Successful interference in the Penitentiary for Juvenile Offenders.

MY own health had suffered severely from the consequences of a very serious carriage accident, and at the time of the marriage of my pupil Hortense I left the palace where I had spent nine years, still remaining on terms of the closest intimacy with all the family, and their guest whenever I came to Paris, returning from the health-resorts where I was sent to undergo medical treatment which lasted several years.

Of course I now heard a great deal as to general opinions in the provinces, where the Empress was severely judged. Her intimacy with the Princess Metternich and other eccentric foreigners, the tone which was admitted at the court, the style of her friends, were bitterly criticized, and often I had to rectify most exaggerated statements. These were reflected in the public papers, in consequence of the greater liberty now conceded to the press. But the effect of misrepresentation was only to make the Empress rebellious and reckless, although in reality she was distressed and grieved, but she became exasperated and only more disposed to indulge in what was blamed.

A great official of the court said to me, earnestly: "If she would only take warning by the example of Marie Antoinette! It is exactly the same history over again. But she will take no hint. My wife tried, but was made to feel that she must not attempt anything of the kind."

The Emperor's private conduct was a constant subject of conversation outside of the court, where only mysterious whispers were heard; but in general society, both in Paris and the provinces, everything was known and freely talked about. The Empress was violently jealous, both with and without cause, multiplying vehement scenes and threatening extreme measures of public scandal. Everything was done to divert her mind. She was first sent to take the waters of Schwalbach, in Germany, where principalities and powers showed her great courtesy, perhaps through motives of benevolent curiosity.

On her return to her imperial home, she was more and more initiated into political questions, which pleased and flattered her by giving importance to her opinion and her judgment. The Empress was extremely intelligent, but also extremely superficial, and had received a very imperfect education. To the last she never learned to write French with grammatical correctness, although her style was natural, spirited, and good in such letters as are known of her inditing. She felt the imperfection of her historical knowledge especially, and its consequences with regard to the political matters which interested her, and caused great surprise by coming to the very sensible decision of taking regular lessons in the history of France from a well-known professor, Fustel de Coulanges.

Having a remarkably good memory, she soon gathered enough to serve her purpose, and often to surprise those with whom she conversed by bringing in examples of her newly acquired knowledge with great adroitness.

There was a strange but very characteristic inconsistency in her proceedings. Now, she was deep in politics, showing a passionate interest in the affairs of the state, and vehemently trying to enforce her views; then, again, she plunged into incessant frivolities with the same interest and a sort of insatiable, restless craving, talking of dress incessantly, as if it were the most important consideration in the world, as it had really become in the society of the court through her example.

Madame Octave Feuillet, in her reminiscences, describes her agonies of anxiety as to her toilet on the occasion of her first dinner at the Tuileries, and the fatigue incurred in conquering difficulties till she reached perfection, all this related as a matter of unavoidable necessity. She had the delight of being addressed at once by the Empress with a compliment on the *chef d'œuvre*, and the request: "You will tell me the name of your 'couturière?'" An explanation followed that the work of art had been performed by Worth, then a budding celebrity, whom the Empress immediately patronized. There is scarcely a court in Europe where a sovereign lady would begin a conversation thus; but, unhappily, the Empress Eugénie had not the early training nor the official reticence of a royal princess. In the same fanciful spirit, her private feelings toward the ministers were too plainly shown in her political intercourse with them. When she liked or disliked the individual, she took no pains to conceal her impressions, which often gave great offense, and caused considerable trouble to the Emperor, who was obliged to salve over wounds which might produce serious complications. There was no possibility of making the Empress understand that such matters had a very different degree of importance from mere society squabbles.

All these "little things" annoyed the Emperor, who also disapproved of her intimacy with Metternich and Nigra; not from personal jealousy, knowing that there was no cause, but for political reasons. It was dangerous for a frank, open-hearted woman, who was too much initiated in the mysteries of the state, to be so very friendly with two wily diplomatists, to whom straws show where the wind blows. Metternich, who was soft and of rather a weak mind, was really fascinated by her attractions, more perhaps than his wife might have approved — especially at first, for the impression seems to have lessened after some time; but Nigra, who played a most enthusiastic part, is currently suspected of having feigned feelings which did not exist, and with very treacherous motives. The Empress was completely deceived, and was convinced that he was absolutely devoted to her. She did not dislike a certain amount of flirtation, keeping at a sufficient distance from the "Rubicon" in all cases; but there was a little too much playing in the neighborhood, perhaps unconsciously, for the Empress was essentially a spotless wife, as she had been a spotless bride, notwithstanding the calumny which assailed her at the time of her extraordinary marriage.

The Duc de Tascher once volunteered to say, when he was relating to me the scene which had taken place between the Emperor, his father, and himself, on the announcement of the former's intentions: "As to the Empress herself, my absolute conviction on my word of honor is that no purer bride ever knelt at the altar. Our objections were not directed against her personally, but on political grounds; and we still think that the Emperor made a great mistake for his future position among the sovereigns of Europe."

THE RUE DE RIVOLI DURING THE BURNING OF THE TUILERIES.

On the right is seen a part of the Tuileries garden, and the Pavillon de Marsan which connected the Tuileries with the north wing of the Louvre.

FROM THE PAINTING BY LÉON Y ESCOSURA

The outbreak of the cholera, and the noble conduct of the Empress, showing the higher side of her complex character, won admiration from her most determined adversaries, so that there was a reaction in her favor, which her friends hoped might be durable.

The act of visiting the cholera hospitals was performed with a degree of resolution and calm courage, which few women in such a position could have shown. She would not allow her ladies to follow her in the hospital wards, but went herself to every one, and, though unaccustomed to such dreadful scenes of suffering, she showed no fear of contagion, taking the patients by the hand, and encouraging all by kind and hopeful words.

At Amiens the disease and deaths had reached frightful proportions. The Empress did not hesitate to go there, for the sole purpose of trying to encourage the population, and stimulate the officials. Here, too, she went to all the beds, and spoke to all without fearing to touch their hands, or to bend over them. One of the officials who accompanied her opened the smallpox ward by mistake, but she insisted on going in and seeing these victims of a hideous disease, like the others. Many women would fear the possible destruction of their beauty, and permanent disfigurement, even more than the risk of life, but this wonderfully beautiful woman quietly performed her adopted mission without fear or hesitation.

The effect on the almost despairing population

was excellent, producing a sort of exhilaration, which at once caused a decrease of the epidemic. The Empress being warmly congratulated by the Bishop on her devotedness and intrepidity, answered very happily and gracefully, in words often quoted since, "Oh, Monseigneur, that is a mere trifle; it is only our way of *standing fire*" (*C'est notre manière d'aller au feu*).

The nature of the Empress Eugénie was high and noble; but what might have been so great and good had been imperfectly developed, and remained ill-regulated under the management of a very worldly mother, who had lived separated from her husband, who became a widow early, and who seems to have had very vague notions of what was desirable for her daughters. The latter were sent from school to school, never remaining long in any, and, when introduced in society, they went from one place to another, in a continual round of amusements, riding about at watering-places, and indulging in a style which was considered — what in modern language is termed — fast. I was conversing on the subject with a Spanish grandee, a young man bearing one of the greatest historical names in Spain.

"Well," he said, "there was nothing wrong, absolutely, but when, for instance, Mademoiselle de Montijo showed herself in public with the bull-fighters [toreadors], at Madrid, it was no sin, but surely it was unsuitable for a young lady of high birth; for she is really a descendant of the Guzmans."

An impetuous nature, utter innocence of intention, and no guidance — such is the explanation of many acts which were so mischievously misinterpreted by the enemies of the Empress Eugénie, before her marriage. The habits thus acquired explain also many of her mistakes when raised to her supreme position. She was in every sense of the word a spoiled child, who had never been restrained in any of her fancies by a mother who was not over-particular or judicious.

The Empress had a large private fortune of her own, but this had been inherited from an uncle who was the head of the Montijo family. The previous years had been full of debt and difficulty in comparatively straitened circumstances, the remembrance of which may have had some influence on the want of generosity which has been attributed to the Empress by those around her. It is only right to add that courtiers are never satisfied, and that I have known many instances which ought to acquit her of such an accusation. But she had not the princely art of giving even trifling marks of remembrance on appropriate occasions, with graceful words of acknowledgment. Opportunities passed, she forgot them, and those who felt neglected were offended.

The Empress Augusta of Germany was celebrated for the manner in which the merest trifles were made valuable by a few gracious words. A ring of small value drawn from her finger, a photograph with a line of writing and her signature — such insignificant offerings were gratefully accepted and preserved as mementos, because the time was well chosen and the act gracefully performed.

The Empress Eugénie could be generous on important occasions, but small things escaped her notice.

With excellent intentions, but without accepting necessary direction from those more experienced than herself, she began to visit hospitals, even without any particular motive for doing so, merely as an act of charity. She went also to prisons and charitable institutions, taking with her only one young lady whom she now had admitted into her household under the name of "reader," but in reality for general utility, as she could claim her services at any time with more freedom than she could use with her ladies in waiting. Mlle. Bouvet, who first filled this post, performed her very unremitting duties with great tact, and gained the favor of the Empress, who afterward, with her habitual love of match-making, made up a marriage with a wealthy agriculturist named Carette,[1] and appointed the bride to a vacant post of lady in waiting. Mlle. Bouvet was remarkably handsome, and in the same style as the Empress Eugénie, though with infinitely less delicacy and refinement in her features and general appearance. Still, she was by no means a safe

---

[1] Mme. Carette has published reminiscences of her life at the imperial court; but necessarily circumstances obliged her to present a picture without shade.

escort for the Empress, as the beauty of both could not but attract attention everywhere. They went together alone, in "Harun al Rashid" style, with only a carriage as a concession to modern requirements, but a vehicle prepared for such occasions, with a coachman and a groom as attendants in dark liveries, and no indication of imperial rank anywhere. With Mlle. Bouvet as her sole protection, the Empress went about, visiting poor families who had been pointed out to her, and even performing various kind offices with her own hands. As usual, the intentions were excellent, the actions ill-judged. Every one who has had anything to do with works of charity in Paris knows the immense risk attending such proceedings for women, and especially young and handsome women. The "ladies of charity" (*dames de charité*) belonging to different charitable societies go only to such houses as are guaranteed to be safe by competent authorities, such as the Sisters of Charity, the parish clergy, or the gentlemen belonging to societies. To all places insufficiently known they go either with Sisters, or at least two together, one being of mature age. There are many parts of Paris where, at that time especially, only male visitors could venture.

The ladies who visit the poor, even now, are always careful to dress in the most ordinary-looking and unfashionable black gowns. The imprudence of two very beautiful and still young women, in the obtrusive dress of the period, going to houses in the

Belleville of that time, filled with the most disreputable people in Paris, may be imagined. The Empress was always fearless to excess, and, leaving her carriage at a distance, without protection of any kind she ran all risks with Mlle. Bouvet, walking through the street to the place she wished to visit. On one occasion she gained some experience at her cost; for, interfering in too imperial fashion with some boys who were quarreling, the mothers took part in the affray, other mothers joined them, and soon the Empress was surrounded by a mob of viragos, in the style of the first Revolution, who abused her in the coarsest language, declaring their very energetic determination of not allowing "ladies in silk dresses" to meddle with them. The Empress soon found that her sole resource was to get back to her carriage as quickly as she could.

With the same kind-hearted inexperience, the Empress greatly annoyed the officials at the head of the hospitals, penitentiaries, etc., by listening too easily to complaints, promising injudicious favors, and with her characteristic vehemence insisting on the immediate execution of difficult reforms.

Every one who has ever watched the working of such institutions knows what caution is required, when touching the machinery, lest more harm than good should result from the disturbance of what is established. Penitentiaries are not intended to be comfortable boarding-houses, where everything is made pleasant to the inmates. All the governors, directors, etc., were exasperated by the charitable impulses of the Empress, and felt strongly inclined to apply the homely phrase of "minding one's own business."

One of her impetuous reforms must, however, be wholly approved, notwithstanding the strong opposition which was shown. The Emperor having gone to Algeria, the Empress was regent during his absence, a measure which was highly unpopular. "Why," was generally objected, "should the Emperor be obliged to appoint a regent when, legally, he has not left France? With modern facilities his orders can be easily transmitted." Why? Because the Empress liked to be regent.

During this period of personal power she went to visit the penitentiary for young offenders. In this establishment five hundred boys from ten to eighteen years of age were kept in solitary confinement. The object put forward was the prevention of criminal contagion; but for young children often arrested only for begging, and retained because they had no decent home to go to, the life was one of moral torture.

The Empress was painfully impressed, and took up the matter with her usual warmth. After conquering considerable opposition, she succeeded in having these children transferred to agricultural penitentiaries, where they work in the open air, and together, under supervision. The results have proved very satisfactory.

CHAPTER XIX

Hints in the papers on the Emperor's health — The cost of a Crown — Visits to provincial towns — Uncomfortable luxury — The true color of the Empress's hair — The great Exhibition — Death of the Emperor Maximilian — Death of the Duc de Tascher and of the Duchesse de Bassano — The Empress goes to the opening of the Suez Canal — Effect on the Mohammedan population — The Emperor and Prince Imperial at Compiègne — My visit to the Tuileries in 1870 — Physical condition of the Emperor — The plebiscite — Testimony of Lord Malmesbury — I leave Paris with sad forebodings — The palace of the Tuileries when I next saw it.

ABOUT this time rumors began to be current as to the total failure of the Emperor's health. Before I left the Tuileries, I had noticed a marked change in his appearance, and this, I was told, had greatly increased. He had grown stouter, but as if puffed; he looked much aged and careworn; and as he walked there was evident suffering, ascribed to rheumatic lameness. The papers hinted that he was seriously ill. Alarmed at all I heard, I wrote to a lady belonging to the court, with whom I was intimate, asking what was the truth. She immediately replied, plainly stating the nature of the malady (as it is known at present), with rheumatic complications, but adding that there was no present danger.[1] She made no

[1] This was at the end of the year 1866.

secret of the matter; so that I have been much surprised to see in various Bonapartist publications the positive assertion that the Empress knew "nothing" of the Emperor's disease till after the fall of the Empire. Sometimes those nearest to the patient are kept in ignorance: still, when so much is public, the case seems strange.

The poor Emperor was subjected to a terrible necessity of self-command at this time. Sovereigns cannot have a headache with impunity; if they are reported to have the least indisposition, stocks fall, a financial commotion occurs, and fortunes are lost in a day. After the most intense suffering, the Emperor appeared at balls and theaters to pacify the public. His rheumatic pains alone were so violent that he was known to hold his arm to the flame of a candle before going into the ball-room, that a change of pain might bring a sort of relief! His prison at Ham was damp and surrounded by a moat; he had always suffered from acute rheumatism since then. But it is well known what a fearful disease was added to this, in his latter years. Those who, for a mere chill, can go to bed comfortably, and ask for soothing drinks, closing their door to all intruders, may understand the suffering of being obliged to appear in public, bearing agonies of pain, with a smile and a gracious word ready for the importunate, concealing physical torture as if it were a sin! Poor potentates! Is a crown worth what it costs?

The Emperor visited several French towns accompanied by the Empress, participating in all festivities prepared for his reception, without betraying any sign of suffering. These visits to provincial towns were always a source of anxiety to the wives of the prefects, who, supposing that royal people could do nothing like others, racked their brains to discover what would be sufficiently worthy of being presented to them. One of these ladies related in my presence that in her anxiety to arrange everything as magnificently as possible, she had prepared the bed for the Empress with richly embroidered sheets. To her surprise, the Empress could not sleep, because the embroidery fretted her peculiarly fine and delicate skin; so the mistress of the house was called up in the night, with a request for plain sheets!

The Empress was extremely simple in her home habits, yet the most ridiculous stories were spread with regard to her supposed luxury. I was told gravely, as an undeniable fact, that from one to two hundred francs' worth of gold dust was used daily to give the golden radiance to her hair!

It so happened that the Duc de Tascher having asked me to tie a lock of hair given to him by the Empress, I had held the hair in my fingers, and had been able to examine it closely. It was beautifully soft and fine, and seemed made up of minute threads apparently of reddish gold, mingled with others equally fine, of a darker color. I could therefore be certain that no artifice was employed; but any impartial observer could have discerned the totally different hue from that produced by hair-dresser's fluids or powders. It was the Venetian auburn of Titian's pictures, with the wonderful complexion usually accompanying that rare shade. The face seemed sculptured in alabaster, the features so delicate as to be almost transparent.

It was beauty so perfect that to be appreciated fully a first glance was not sufficient. The more the whole form of the Empress was examined, the more the observer felt that it could not be surpassed, and was rarely equaled. There were peculiarities, but no defects.

Notwithstanding some threatening whispers, the apparent prosperity of the Empire continued to increase without interruption till the year of the Great Exhibition of 1867, when all the sovereigns of Europe came to Paris to be the guests of Napoleon III., as their fathers had done during 1811, in the reign of the founder of the dynasty. But, as in 1811, this culminating point of prosperity was not to be reached with impunity. There was nothing beyond, and the terrible downfall was at hand.

The first note of the knell was rung by the death of Maximilian, the news of which reached the Emperor on the very day when, in all his glory, he distributed the prizes of the Great Exhibition. He was deeply affected, but the fact was concealed till the ceremony was over, when all festivities were stopped.

It was an ominous ending to such rejoicings.

The death of the young Comtesse de l'Espine (Hortense de Tascher) had occurred in the beginning of the year, a fortnight after the birth of her daughter, and had destroyed on my part any wish even to look at scenes of gaiety or pleasure. The Duc de Tascher soon followed her by a most sudden and startling catastrophe, immediately after giving orders to his valet with regard to preparations for a state ball in the evening, where he was to attend the Empress. I was not in Paris at the time, and was deeply shocked and grieved, for I had always found in him a kind friend.

The Duchesse de Bassano was taken, also, in that fatal year following the Exhibition, after a few hours of illness. She was an immense loss, not only to her broken-hearted husband and children, but to the Empress, to whom she was a devoted friend who would have followed her anywhere, for "weal or woe," according to the traditions so faithfully retained by all the family de Bassano.

I was deeply attached to the Duchesse de Bassano,—the best of friends and the most excellent of women,—withal the *grande dame*, from head to foot, blending the most perfect dignity with the most attractive simplicity and natural grace of manner. I often thought, when I saw her in full dress, that she would make an ideal empress or queen; but at all times, at all hours, in her own home or in her court functions, there was something that rendered familiarity impossible even to the most ill-bred, and at the same time a gentle sweetness which attracted and gave confidence to the most timid. It was perfect high breeding with perfect kindness.

The sudden death of Comte Walewski, which soon followed, was a great blow to the Emperor. One by one his most valued friends and counselors were taken from him at the time when he most required their aid, for his health was evidently failing more and more, notwithstanding official denials.

In 1869 the inauguration of the Suez Canal seemed to call for the presence of the Emperor, who had patronized the work from the first, as a national undertaking, and by a timely grant of money had saved it from the fate which awaited Panama after his death. He felt, however, that he could not risk the journey, but yielded to the ardent wish of the Empress by sending her as his representative. All those competent to judge the question considered that this concession was an immense mistake in a Mohammedan country, where no one could understand that a woman should act as a representative of her husband, and go about publicly as such, when, according to the feelings of the natives, the mere act of appearing without a veil is positively immodest.

As usual, the Empress would listen to no advice, and leaving without hesitation her husband and son, she went off, in state, on her adventurous expedition, at great cost, and with general disapprobation. When she reached Constantinople, she went at first to the French Embassy, which was her proper home; but she did not like Pera, where the surroundings were not sufficiently Oriental to satisfy her fancy and her curiosity. Consequently, she took the extraordinary decision of accepting an offer of hospitality from the Sultan, and residing at his palace.

A gentleman who was at Constantinople during the visit of the Empress told me that the consternation of all the Europeans was indescribable, and the lamentable effect on the Orientals likewise, who attributed to the worst possible motives an act which simply sprang from curiosity, but which, in their eyes, outraged all propriety. That any woman who did not belong to the seraglio should voluntarily live under the same roof as the Sultan, was inadmissible in their sight; even the seraglio is kept apart, and is not on the easy terms which were established for the Empress, in defiance of all Oriental custom. But in this, as in so many other imprudent acts, there was complete innocence of intention, and nothing more worthy of blame than thoughtless levity. In the last years of the Empire, the moral intoxication of all the women of fashion, begun by the Princess Metternich, was daily increasing; each one daring more than the others, till all conventional rules of propriety were despised and trodden under foot. The Empress was not exempt from this fatal influence — the atmosphere she breathed was bad. "The style of the women around her is vile," says Lord Malmesbury in his memoirs; thus giving the impression of a friendly Englishman, who fully appreciated all that was charming and really good in the Empress, but deplored certain drawbacks.

While the sovereign lady was thus enjoying her fanciful journey, and startling the propriety of Turks and Egyptians, the Emperor, fearing dullness for his young son in the empty Compiègne, invited a few intimates, and with his usual self-control and unselfishness showed such cheerfulness, and took so much trouble to amuse his guests and the young Prince, that he seemed indefatigable, leading the games himself and tiring everybody before showing any symptoms of personal fatigue. Every one was satisfied that nothing serious could ail him; and yet the truth is now too well known as to the deadly disease, which was even then so terribly developed. Surgeons had already urged the necessity of an operation, but he had a nervous dread of such means of cure, and had concealed the fact from the Empress, knowing that, with her characteristic determined spirit, she would have insisted on the operation being performed and would not easily have been silenced.

The Emperor had unexpectedly granted liberal reforms, for which the French nation was perhaps not sufficiently prepared; he probably felt that his hand was no longer able to hold the reins.

I came to Paris early in the spring of the fatal year 1870: but accompanying a friend, with whom I was staying. I therefore did not live at the Tuileries on this occasion, but went there immediately after my arrival. I was, as usual, warmly received;

but, after some conversation, one of the ladies of the family said to me: "We are very anxious on the Emperor's account. He is certainly very ill, and has fallen into a state of apathy and torpor which is most unnatural. He seems indifferent to everything. Just like Charles," she added, in a low voice, alluding to the late Duke, who, for some time before his death, seemed in the same dreamy state as that attributed to the Emperor. I had watched this symptom in the case of the Duke with considerable alarm; but the family did not see its importance. The servants had given me some particulars of his health, which seemed to point to disease not identical with that of the Emperor, but of the same nature, and producing the same unnatural depression.

On one occasion when the court circle was playing at the "society" game which asks questions as to tastes, habits, preferences, etc., in answer to an inquiry as to his favorite occupation, the Emperor wrote: "Chercher la solution de problèmes insolubles" (Seeking the solution of insoluble problems). The problems were more insoluble than ever, and the Emperor had no longer the strength to seek a solution. In his evident anxiety as to what was coming, he provoked an appeal to the nation — a plebiscite — to confirm the liberalized constitution granted by the Emperor, which was approved by above 7,000,000 votes.

I remember the excitement and enthusiasm in

GALLERY OF PEACE, RUINS OF THE TUILERIES.
FROM A PHOTOGRAPH

Paris when the result was known. Every one would have supposed that the future of the Empire was secured indefinitely.

Lord Malmesbury mentions that he came to Paris at this time; and, speaking of the Emperor, he says:

"I found him much altered in appearance, and looking very ill, it being three years since I had seen him. . . . He observed later that Europe appeared to be tranquil; and it was evident to me that at that moment he had no idea of the coming hurricane which suddenly broke out in the first week of the following July. . . . I feel sure that not a thought of the impending idea of a Hohenzollern being a candidate for the Spanish throne had crossed his mind. Count Bismarck had kept it a profound secret, and that very deep secrecy and sudden surprise is the strongest proof of his intention to force a quarrel upon France. . . . The result of my visit and conversation with the Emperor was one of extreme pain, for I saw that he was no longer the same man of sanguine energy and self-reliance, and had grown prematurely old and broken."

This account by Lord Malmesbury, who, as a very old friend of the Emperor from almost boyish days, was particularly interested in all concerning him, absolutely confirms all that I heard myself during my stay in Paris.

At the Tuileries, in the apartments of the de Tascher family, all was sad in consequence of the Duke's death, which had occurred in the preceding year. The Emperor had desired the ladies to retain the apartments until the death of the (Princess) Countess, whom he wished to leave undisturbed; but every one felt that the fatal time was not far distant. I found her much broken; and at over eighty years of age everything was to be feared. She received me most affectionately, repeating how much she missed me, and that she could not get accustomed to my absence, adding earnestly: "Come and drive with me in the Bois de Boulogne, as we used to do." I went with her, feeling painfully that it would be the last time.[1]

My old friend Robert was now filling his father's place and enjoying his honors. This, too, seemed strange and painful, though it was impossible to be more heartily friendly than he showed himself on that occasion, as on all others.

I left the palace with sorrowful forebodings — a sort of threatening cloud seemed to hang over it, nay, over Paris itself. As I saw Paris recede in the distance on the day of my departure, I thought of the doomed cities in Scripture, and my impression was so deep that I even expressed my fears in a letter to a relative in America, who was greatly struck when events so terribly justified what then seemed to be almost prophetic views.

The next time that I stood before the palace of the Tuileries, it was in ruins! I could still discover the

---

[1] She died at the château of one of her daughters, in Alsace, at the beginning of the war, which was concealed from her.

remains of my old apartments, which I longed to visit, but was told that the danger would be too great. I could discern what was left of the "Salle des Maréchaux," where I had witnessed such splendid scenes of festivity. I could still see the place where had been my habitual seat in that chapel where my loved Hortense had been married, in the presence of Napoleon III. and the Empress Eugénie!

The Archbishop of Paris, who then officiated, had been foully murdered; the fair young bride was in her grave; the Duke, her father, who had led her to the altar, was no more; the Emperor and Empress were exiles; and the very chapel where she had knelt, with her bridal veil and wreath of orange blossoms, was in ruins!

Who would wonder at the tears which I could not repress?

CHAPTER XX

Apathy of the Emperor—The party of the Empress—A consultation of medical and surgical authorities on the Emperor's health—An operation declared necessary—The Hohenzollern incident—The Emperor unwilling for war—The scene at St. Cloud related to Lord Malmesbury by the Duc de Gramont—The Emperor yields—His sad forebodings—The Empress appointed Regent—The Prince Imperial goes with his father to join the army—The "baptism of fire"—First reverses—The Empress returns to Paris—The Emperor's health gives way—He is urged to return to Paris—Opposition of the Empress—The Emperor sends the Prince Imperial to Belgium—The Emperor goes to Sedan against his will—The Prince Imperial receives orders to go over to England, where he meets his mother at Hastings.

THE torpor of the Emperor exasperated the Empress, who did not understand its cause, and she strove with passionate expostulations to rouse him to his former vigor of purpose. His mind and intellect had not failed, but his physical energies had given way so completely that the former seemed dormant. There was now a political party calling itself "le parti de l'Impératrice" (the party of the Empress), and the ministers, with other politicians, perpetually held consultations with her, talking her over to their views, which she then enforced in vehement scenes with the exhausted, weary Emperor.

Lord Malmesbury says again:

"My impression as to his having given a constitutional government to France was that it was more the result of bodily suffering and exhaustion from a deadly disease than from any moral conviction, and that he felt, as he must have done, that the life left him was short, and that his son would have a better chance of quietly inheriting the throne under a parliamentary and irresponsible *régime*. Perhaps he was right, if he had found able ministers; but that was not the case, and their mismanagement at the provocations of Prussia under Bismarck must always be cited as the most incapable diplomacy on record."

Shortly before these fatal incidents, rumors concerning the Emperor's health became so alarming that the Duchesse de Mouchy (Princess Anna Murat) urged the Empress to have a consultation with several celebrated surgical and medical authorities, presided over by the famous Dr. Germain Sée. The statement of the case was duly drawn up by Dr. Sée, declaring the now well-known nature of the malady, and the urgent necessity of an operation. The friends of the Empress assert positively that the truth was concealed from her, and that she remained ignorant of the true state of the Emperor.

Immediately after this consultation, the Hohenzollern incident occurred suddenly. It was of a nature to excite passionate feelings in the Empress, for it concerned Spain, giving the crown of Spain to a

German prince. Now (since the war which followed has caused such calamities) the partizans of the Empress deny strenuously that she was in favor of risking it, or that she ever used the words so often quoted: "This is my war." It is, however, certain on the best authority that she considered any concession on the French side to be disgraceful, and that she took up the question with her usual passionate vehemence and direct interference. We must again quote Lord Malmesbury:

"The Duke himself [de Gramont[1]] gave me the following account of the last scene on July 14, before the declaration of war.

"The Hohenzollern candidateship to the throne of Spain was abandoned, and the Emperor was decidedly disposed to accept this renouncement and to patch up the quarrel and turn this result into a diplomatic success, but his ministers had avoided no opportunity of publishing the insult[2] to all France, and the press stirred the anger and vanity of the public to a pitch of madness. None had yet taken advantage of the characteristic temper of the Emperor. Before the final resolve to declare war, the Emperor, Empress, and ministers went to St. Cloud. After some discussion, Gramont told me, the Empress, a high-spirited and impressionable woman, made a strong and most excited address, declaring that war

[1] Then Minister of Foreign Affairs.
[2] The telegram, now acknowledged to be false by Prince Bismarck, which was sent by him over Europe, and which represented that the King of Prussia had refused to receive the French ambassador.

'was inevitable if the honor of France was to be sustained.' She was immediately followed by Marshal Lebœuf, who in the most violent tone threw down his portfolio and swore that if war was not declared he would give it up and renounce his military rank. The Emperor gave way, and Gramont went straight to the Chamber to announce the fatal news."

This narrative was confirmed by another, given to me personally on good authority. The latter states that the Emperor positively refused to sign the declaration of war, and left the room, after the scene with the Empress and Marshal Lebœuf. The former showed great anger, and seizing the arm of one of the ministers, she exclaimed against the apathy of the Emperor, adding: "We will make him do it!" She followed the weary Emperor, who finally yielded to her pressing insistence.

The Empress no doubt attributed the Emperor's opposition to the physical languor and unwillingness for exertion which had characterized his conduct for some time, and thought it necessary to use energetic means to rouse him from his torpor. But the responsibility was an awful one in the case of a woman not called by duty to take such a decision as a reigning sovereign.

When war was declared, and she saw how gravely and sadly the Emperor looked toward the future, she was herself frightened at the sight of the demon which she had raised, and would gladly have welcomed any peaceful intervention—but it was too late. The Emperor went to the war with the worst forebodings, and with the despairing resignation of a doomed victim. Let those who accuse him of having rashly and presumptuously undertaken the task under which he fell read the sad proclamation at the beginning of the campaign, and compare it with the spirited resolution which announced the Italian war —that war which was a triumphant march through Lombardy, crowned by the glorious victory of Solferino. What a departure from the Tuileries was that, and what a return! Alas! that magnificent success had taught the French nation to believe itself invincible, and led to the fatal delusion of 1870 —a delusion which, however, was not shared by the Emperor, who seemed to feel that his day was come.

His own departure for the army was caused by characteristic sentimental motives of "sharing the fate of his soldiers"; but in his physical state it was an act of folly. For a considerable time he had been unable to ride a horse without intense suffering; he was utterly incapable physically of acting as commander-in-chief; and his presence prevented any of the marshals from being appointed to that supreme command.

His resolution of taking with him the Prince Imperial, then only fourteen years of age, was much blamed, notwithstanding the sonorous terms in which it was announced. Every one expressed the sensible view of the matter, viz., that the place of a school-boy was in the school-room, and not with an army in active service, which would entail fatigue and risk beyond the physical powers of his age.

But the real truth was concealed. It was considered safer for the boy to be with his father in the French army than to be exposed to the risk of being seized, perhaps, as a hostage by a revolutionary mob, should there be riots in Paris.

When the Empress was first appointed Regent during the Italian war, the Emperor was blamed for giving the government of France "into the hands of a mere woman of fashion." But if he had not yielded to the ardent wish of the Empress, he would have had no one whom he could appoint to the office but Prince Napoleon, who was universally unpopular, and who had, besides, a sort of Richard the Third flavor about him, which caused the most vehement opposition on the part of the Empress and of many among the Emperor's most trusted advisers. In 1870 the mistake, now universally acknowledged, lay in going with the army instead of appointing a responsible commander-in-chief. Unfortunately, the Empress was blind as to his present condition, and with her high and romantic feelings she considered that he ought to lead his army, refusing to see any impediments. Consequently she was naturally appointed Regent, as before.

The Emperor did not join the army from Paris, or leave officially, as he had done in 1859 for the Italian war. He evidently dreaded the fatigue of popular demonstrations, which was in itself a proof of his weakened state, and started from St. Cloud, reaching the army by cross railway lines. The poor little Prince, delighted with his uniform as sub-lieutenant, and his sword, which he proudly grasped tight, was yet struggling to keep back natural childish tears as he looked up into his mother's face and held her hand. She preserved perfect self-command as she embraced her husband and son; and when the train moved off she called to the boy: "Louis, do your duty!"

What the military duty of such a child could be is not easily comprehensible, and most people would have liked her better if, instead of heroic speeches, she had shown more natural tenderness. When the train had disappeared round the curve of the line, and she had seen the last look, the last wave of the hand, from both husband and son,—then only,—she wept.

The Empress Eugénie was too fond of being sublime.

The first telegram from the Emperor, after the first successful skirmish of Saarbrück, "Louis has had the *baptism of fire*," was much ridiculed by those who did not know that the expression is habitually used in French, meaning that a soldier has stood fire well for the first time. The poor boy had not flinched, though the shot fell around him. He had "done his duty," and was laughed at, which stung the Empress to the quick.

I was at Granville, a small seaport in Normandy, with a friend, when the war broke out.

Who can forget that war?—the bewildering succession of defeats—the astonishment and fury of the French nation as each telegram came!

I remember that rumors having reached me of a great catastrophe (the defeat of Wörth or Reichshofen), I went out to see the telegram pasted upon the walls in the little town. A crowd of fishermen and their wives were gathered round it, evidently trying in vain to decipher the appalling news. I drew near. An old fishwife then said to me: "Madame, you who can read—will you not read it to us?"

Of course I immediately acquiesced, and raising my voice I read the fatal telegram relating the defeat of the French army, but concluding with words of hope. The consternation of those around me seemed to accept no comfort; they looked at each other in blank despair.

As I moved away, I remembered with increasing anxiety what the old Comte de Tascher had said to me in the beginning of the Italian war: "Everything depends on the success of the first battle. If our troops are victorious, the campaign will be triumphant; but the French cannot bear defeat."

Alas! the war of 1870 began with a defeat, and the old General's words were verified.

The unfortunate Empress then left St. Cloud for the Tuileries, where she established a field hospital, and there she received day by day the war bulletins, which became more and more alarming.

The Emperor's health had given way completely in the very beginning of the war. The fatigue, the absence of medical care, had increased his sufferings to an unendurable degree, and he had been obliged to hand over the command of the Army of Châlons to Marshal MacMahon, who, after the disasters, very nobly declared that he was alone responsible, and that he had acted against the views and wishes of the Emperor, who no longer commanded the army. The presence of the Emperor was not only of no possible use, but was, in fact, an impediment to due rapidity of movement, etc.; and all the marshals, generals, and superior officers were of opinion that he ought to return to Paris, taking with him a sufficient portion of the army to cover Paris, and thus, protected by the forts which surround the fortifications, render the advance of the Germans too perilous to be attempted. Prince Napoleon was energetically in favor of this plan, and especially of the Emperor's return; the latter himself agreed that his proper place was at the head of the government in Paris itself.

But the Empress vehemently opposed his return, declaring that a revolution would break out if the Emperor appeared in Paris after defeat; that he would be accused of personal cowardice, with a selfish wish to concentrate the troops round his own person for the interests of the dynasty. The best proof of the weakened state of the unhappy Emperor is shown by the mere fact of his taking her will to account, instead of appearing in Paris without even consulting her, as he would have done a few years before that time.

Who was right, who was wrong, in such appreciations?

Opinions are divided; but the most reliable and authorized blame the Empress for taking such a responsibility against the opinions of the generals who, being on the spot, were certainly better able to judge what ought to be done than she could, at the Tuileries, with her advisers. Trochu was sent to Paris with the mission to the Empress, of explaining how matters stood, and to urge the necessity of the Emperor's return; but she would listen to no argument, and the unfortunate Emperor remained with the army, a mere burden, repulsed on all sides; while the Empress, without even consulting him, governed Paris, summoning the Legislative Assembly without his authorization, changing her ministers (whose advice she would not follow), and sending orders to the army commanders disconcerting their plans.

It is unnecessary to explain that the writer of these pages has not the presumption either to express, or even to form, an opinion on such a momentous subject. The Empress acted according to her views and convictions; it is for others to judge whether she was right or wrong. Her most zealous partizans, however, reluctantly admit that she was mistaken in her opposition to the Emperor's return, and deplore that she did not leave the responsibility of such a decision to those better qualified to bear the load.

With the resignation of a victim, the Emperor, though disapproving the march on Sedan, and foreseeing the consequences, yet followed the army; having reached such a degree of suffering, both physical and moral, that the one hope left to him was in the mercy of death by a shot on the field of battle. But the poor young Prince Imperial, whose health had completely given way, imperatively required rest and care which he could not have in a camp, and the Emperor, who wished to spare him the sight of what would follow according to his previsions, sent the young Prince to Mézières, promising to summon him to Sedan.

But, after several contradictory telegrams, which drove him vainly to and fro, positive orders were received to cross the Belgian frontier at once, which was effected without informing the Prince of the motives for this determination, or even where the train was taking him.

On the frontier the dreadful truth was revealed to the poor boy, who had struggled so hard to behave manfully "like a soldier"—to "do his duty," as his mother had said, and who now broke down completely, like the child he really was, repeating with bitter tears and sobs: "My poor father! Our army! Poor France!"

He was taken to Namur, where the Prince de Chimay, governor of the province, received him with every kindness and care at the Château de Chimay.

But a telegram came, signed by the Emperor:

"I am the King of Prussia's prisoner. Take the Prince to England."

And the poor, weary boy, crushed and heartbroken, set off again for Ostend, whence he crossed over to Dover and Hastings, where he met his mother, whom he had left, little more than a month before, with such bright hopes of glory—so proud to "be a soldier"—so anxious to "do his duty"!

CHAPTER XXI

MacMahon leads the army to Sedan — Despair of the Emperor — He vainly seeks death — He gives up his sword to the King of Prussia — Telegram to the Empress — Confusion and treachery around her — The Princess Clotilde comes to share her danger — The ambassadors of Austria and Italy offer their protection — She goes with them, followed only by Madame Lebreton — The Empress and Madame Lebreton left to their fate in a hackney-carriage.

WHEN, obeying orders from the Regency in Paris, MacMahon, in the vain hope of joining Bazaine, turned his army corps toward Sedan,— a town situated in a hollow surrounded by hills,—the unfortunate Emperor clearly foresaw what must happen, and in his despair thought only of seeking death, yet he was too much of a believer to commit the crime of suicide.

For five consecutive hours he remained in the saddle—an effort which, under the circumstances, the surgeons who attended him declared to have been superhuman; he exposed his person on the most dangerous points, where he repeatedly went forward alone, with shells and shot falling round him, hoping to find there the end of his torture, without himself destroying his own life. At last, unscarred, but

RUINS OF THE HALL OF THE MARSHALS, CARYATIDES OF THE THRONE ON THE RIGHT.

FROM A PHOTOGRAPH.

having reached the last point of exhaustion, annihilated by pain and grief, he returned to the town of Sedan, where the army was crowding in the greatest confusion. As the shells fell into the streets, full of wounded and fugitive soldiers, the destruction took the proportions of a massacre. MacMahon was severely wounded, and unable to give orders. All was confusion. The Emperor then ordered the white flag to be hoisted above the town. It was not immediately perceived, and the firing continued, while the Emperor, in a state of prostration, as if in a delirious dream, repeated: "They are still firing! The cannon! The cannon! It must be stopped! It must be stopped!"

At last the signal was noticed, the firing was interrupted, and the Emperor sent his well-known message to the King of Prussia:

"Having been unable to meet death at the head of my troops, I give up my sword to Your Majesty."

The rest is too well known to need description: The personal surrender of the unfortunate Emperor, the pitiless terms of the conquering Germans, a whole army carried off as prisoners.

It is evident that if the Emperor had retained any remnant of his former energies, matters would never have reached such a disastrous extremity, and that, like Francis Joseph of Austria after Solferino, he would have sought peace before that time, when the exigencies of the Germans would have been far less heavy than they proved at a later period, after the insane resistance carried on by Gambetta, who was so generous in shedding the blood of others (not even his countrymen, for he was a Genoese), driving the French like a flock of sheep to the shambles.

The Empress had remained at the Tuileries in constant consultation with the ministers, in an agony of hope and fear, but still preserving delusions, still believing that one blow struck at the proper time would change the course of events. But, day by day, the war bulletins became more appalling, till at last a telegram was given to her:

"The army is vanquished, and in captivity. I am myself a prisoner.   "NAPOLEON."

What the suffering of the following night must have been to the Empress is beyond imagination. Here was a wife and mother in the responsible position of Regent, left to face the hatred of an exasperated mob, who, not unjustly, attributed the disastrous war to her influence. She had said, or was believed to have said, "This is *my* war," and those unfortunate words will never be forgotten or forgiven in France. The constant prosperity of the Empire had deluded her into the belief that it would always continue. She had looked forward to glory, to increase of territory, to the gratitude of the nation; and she had only provoked a series of calamities such as the French had never yet seen. Now all hope was gone; but still she could not immediately realize the consequences of the Emperor's position, and she could not imagine that in the very presence of the conquerors the nation would reject its unhappy sovereign. Her first words on hearing the terrible news had been, "Do not think of me — think of France"; but France and the Empire still seemed to her inseparable.

During the whole night ministers, senators, politicians, and deputies were coming and going, to and fro, from the Tuileries. All was confusion. Some remained, resting as they could in arm-chairs or on sofas, while servants brought refreshments.

The Empress refused to take any rest, notwithstanding the entreaties of her attendants. At seven o'clock on the morning of the fatal fourth of September (Sunday) she heard mass in her private oratory for the last time, and then received the ministers and General Trochu, the governor of Paris, who had said to her: "Madame, I am a Catholic, a Breton — a soldier — and I will die at your feet sooner than harm shall reach you!"

On that eventful morning he seemed still devoted to her, and discussed the measures to be taken for preserving order and putting down any insurrection, expressing to his colleagues the greatest admiration for her energy.

A few hours later, General Trochu was at the head of the Provisional Government at the Hôtel de Ville, while the Empress Eugénie was left to her fate. And yet the man was not a traitor. He was a talker, fond of making sonorous speeches, saying more than he meant, and then forgetting what he had said, full of good intentions, but also full of vanity, considering himself indispensable to the safety of the nation, and sincerely convinced that all, including his promised allegiance to the Empress, must be sacrificed to the general good.

Meanwhile, the progress of events was fearfully rapid. Every half-hour brought more disastrous news. The Chamber of Deputies had been invaded by the mob; the downfall of the Empire had been decreed; the Republic had been proclaimed. The cries of the popular fury were heard in the very gardens of the Tuileries, and the enraged populace was coming nearer and nearer. The crowd reached the reserved garden in front of the palace, and tore down the emblematic imperial eagles. It was then a quarter past three in the afternoon.

The Austrian and Italian ambassadors, who were at the palace (with other supposed friends of the Empire, and some sincere adherents), now entreated her to leave the dangerous imperial home, but she warmly rejected the proposal. She was the daughter of a noble race; the heroic blood of the Guzmans, her Spanish ancestors, flowed in her veins; and she could not but consider flight as an act of cowardice. She "was a sentinel left to defend a post, and she would die there."

The roar of the mob became louder and louder, the cries of "Vive la République!" were distinctly heard.

"Madame," then said the prefect of police, Pietri, "by remaining here you will cause a general massa-ere of all your attendants." She seemed struck by this, and turning to General Mellinet, she said: "Can you defend the palace without bloodshed?"

"Madame, I fear that it would be impossible."

"Then all is over," said the Empress. She turned to those present: "Gentlemen, can you bear me witness that I have done my duty to the last?"

They hastily answered, "Yes," still urging her to leave the palace, while the two ambassadors protested that if she would go with them, they would answer for her safety under their protection. As they had long been on terms of friendship with her, and had always made great demonstrations of personal attachment, the Empress trusted them without remembering that the first consideration in the sight of diplomatists is the interest of their respective courts.

Let me hasten to add that her ever-faithful friend and follower, the Duc de Bassano, was not there; he was at the Senate-house vainly trying to stem the flood. Had he been within reach, he would never have left her to the exclusive care of aliens, however distinguished in rank and position. The Duc de Tascher, who was so completely devoted to her cause, and who would have been able to make his voice heard with authority in any presence, had died two years before, and no one present dared to take the lead as to deciding what she ought to do, although the rapidly increasing danger of her situation was evident to all.

In the midst of this agitation and perplexity the Princess Clotilde appeared, coming from the Palais Royal, with her usual quiet resolution, prepared to share whatever danger might threaten the Empress. The latter immediately told her what had been proposed, and urged her not to remain in Paris. After the decision of the Empress had been made known to her, the Princess Clotilde retired, and prepared for her own departure, which she effected in royal fashion with all her accustomed state, and without the slightest opposition from the mob, who treated her with the greatest respect as she passed, perfectly calm as usual, on her way to the Lyons station in her well-known carriage.

Meanwhile, the Empress bade farewell to all her attendants of the "service d'honneur," who were assembled in the rose-colored room—a fairy bower, ill suited as a frame for such a tragic picture, and which she was never to see again.

No one knew where she was going—no one even inquired. The two ladies who were especially "in waiting" asked if they were to follow her, but she refused, saying that she would involve no one in her evil fortunes. Some writers have described in most romantic fashion these last scenes, representing the Empress as a sort of tragic queen, surrounded by weeping and devoted attendants, and making grand sonorous speeches to her ministers and ladies, bidding them farewell in the style of the final scene in Schiller's "Mary Stuart." The Empress was brave and resolute, but she was not and could not be perfectly calm and self-possessed in such a situation, with danger increasing every moment, and conflicting advice all around her. I have heard the Empress taxed with cowardice for her flight. But the bravest military commanders, who fear nothing on the battle-field, shrink from falling into the power of a lawless mob. The Empress had been warned that evils worse than death awaited her, and of these a woman cannot, and ought not, to accept the risk. The Empress had lived in a state of overwrought nerves and physical fatigue for some time; to obtain even a little sleep, she had been obliged to have recourse to narcotics; she had not even gone to bed on the previous night, and had hardly tasted food. How could she be calm and collected under such circumstances? She was not in the habit, at any time, of indulging in eloquent speeches; she often expressed romantic, rather high-flown, thoughts or maxims, but she always spoke in short, abrupt sentences, rather disconnected, without any affectation.

There was no time for eloquence on this occasion. She says herself in one of her published letters: "Trochu forsook me, if not worse; he never appeared at the Tuileries after the Chamber [of Deputies] was invaded by the mob any more than the ministers, with the exception of three, who urged me to leave."[1]

---

[1] "Le Général Trochu m'a abandonnée, *si ce n'est pire* ; il n'a jamais paru aux Tuileries après l'envahissement de la Chambre pas plus que le ministère, à l'exception de trois ministres, qui ont insisté pour mon départ."

The haste of her departure was so great that she had not even time to finish the packing of a small hand-bag containing a few necessaries, which was found in her private room on a table, half filled and left open. Two of her ladies hastily assisted her to put on a long cloak, a close bonnet, and a thick veil; Madame Canrobert offered her carriage, but the Empress seemed hardly to understand, and appeared as if dazed, merely bidding a hasty good-by to all.

All present were bewildered and uncertain as to what they ought to do, fully supposing that under the protection of the two ambassadors she would be perfectly safe, and so accustomed to court reticence and submission that they did not venture to oppose what seemed to be her wishes, or to ask any questions as to her intentions. One lady, who filled a secondary, though confidential post in the household—Madame Lebreton (sister to General Bourbaki)—would not leave her unhappy mistress, and resolutely followed her into exile. With this one faithful attendant, and the two ambassadors, the Empress threaded the galleries communicating with the Louvre, while the mob broke into the Tuileries on the other side. There was a door of communication, which was found locked, and for one brief moment anxiety was intense; happily, the key was quickly procured through a faithful servant, and crossing the splendid gallery of Apollo in the Louvre, the fugitives made their way into the place opposite the church of St. Germain l'Auxerrois.

Two crowds of insurgents were coming in different directions; the danger was great, and the Austrian ambassador, Prince Metternich, went off in haste to seek his carriage, which he had left on the quay at a great distance! Meanwhile, a street boy called out, "There is the Empress!" Much alarmed, the Italian ambassador, Chevalier Nigra, hastily thrust the Empress and Madame Lebreton into a hackney-cab, called to the coachman, "*Boulevard Haussmann*," without giving any number, and turned to silence the boy. The driver, frightened at the approach of the mob, drove off in violent haste, and the two ambassadors immediately lost sight of the vehicle.

It appears now to be certain, from state papers recently revealed, that treaties of alliance had been drawn up between France, Italy, and Austria. The promised aid of Italy was conditional on that of Austria, who declared herself to be unable to finish preparations before September. The flight of the Regent on the fourth of September, and the establishment of a revolutionary government, at once released the powers from promises which after the reverses of the French became particularly inconvenient to fulfil. The immense interest of the ambassadors in getting rid of the Empress is evident; but in any case it is impossible to exonerate them from the grossest mismanagement, if not cowardice, or even treachery.

CHAPTER XXII

The Empress applies to Dr. Evans in her distress — Leaves Paris in his carriage — A perilous journey — The arrival at Trouville — Sir John Burgoyne and his sailing-yacht, the *Gazelle* — Consents to take the Empress over to England — A perilous undertaking — Tremendous storm — Safe arrival at Ryde — The Empress meets her son at Hastings — Hires a furnished country house at Chiselhurst — The Emperor a prisoner at Wilhelmshöhe — His patience and kindness.

THE Empress had no money about her, and when, on reaching a quieter region, the driver asked where he was to take her, she knew not whither to go. Several calls were made at the houses of friends; none were at home, and the Empress, utterly exhausted and not knowing where to find a refuge, suddenly remembered that Dr. Evans, the well-known American dentist, lived near, and to him she went. Dr. Evans was about to go to dinner, and at first refused to see the unknown lady who came at such an unpropitious time; but as she insisted upon speaking to him, he came out, and was struck with astonishment on finding himself in the presence of the fugitive Empress. To his honor be it said that never in the days of imperial prosperity could she have met with more respect or more devoted zeal in her service than was shown on this occasion by Dr. Evans, and afterward by Mrs. Evans, who was at Trouville for sea-bathing, and consequently could not assist her husband in receiving his unexpected imperial guest in Paris. But nothing that could be done for her comfort was neglected, and at least she felt safe in the shelter of the American home. The most important question, however, still remained to be settled — what was she to do, and where was she to go?

Dr. Evans was inclined to advise the railway to Belgium,[1] which she could have reached in a few hours, but the Empress was convinced that she would be recognized and given over to the Revolutionists; consequently, after much discussion, it was settled that she should first take the rest so sorely needed, and that on the next morning she and her faithful attendant should leave Paris with Dr. Evans in his carriage; then with the help of hired vehicles and horses they would contrive to reach Trouville, where they would find Mrs. Evans and her hospitable care, while Dr. Evans would seek means to take them over to England.

The plan was full of peril for all those concerned, but happily it was carried out successfully.

On the morning of the fifth of September, the Empress with Madame Lebreton and Dr. Evans, in his car-

---

[1] The new Prefect of Police, Comte de Kératry, supposing that the Empress would choose the line leading to Belgium, had sent detectives to protect her; so that, in fact, she would have encountered far less danger than in her long journey to Trouville.

riage, drove to the Neuilly gate of Paris, not without considerable anxiety as to the possibility of passing through without recognition; but when Dr. Evans leaned out of the carriage, speaking with an unmistakable Anglo-American accent, no suspicion was awakened, and they passed safely. As they left Paris the Empress wept bitterly.

A fatiguing journey followed, with many difficulties, changes of vehicles and horses, and fear of recognition in the towns where they were obliged to stop. It is stated that in one of her characteristic moments of impulse, the Empress, seeing a policeman ill use a man in the street at Lisieux, started up in her carriage, forgetting her present situation, and exclaimed: "I am the Empress, and I command you to let that man go." Dr. Evans, naturally much alarmed, drew her back to her seat, and explained to the bystanders that she was insane, and that he was her medical attendant, taking care of her, with the assistance of a maid. This story was maintained through the journey, also at the hotel of Trouville, where he took her to Mrs. Evans, who had furnished apartments there. But it is, indeed, wonderful that she was not recognized, her face being so remarkable and so well known.

The fugitives did not reach Trouville-Deauville till the sixth of September at midday; and Dr. Evans at once began to seek means of taking the Empress over to England. A small sailing-yacht, the *Gazelle*, belonging to Sir John Burgoyne, had been for some days lying alongside the quay of Deauville,[1] after cruising along the coast; and the weather being very stormy, did not intend to leave immediately.

Dr. Evans went on board with his nephew, and sending his card to Sir John Burgoyne, explained to him that the Empress of the French was concealed in the town; that she was in trouble and danger; begging him to take her on board at once. Sir John Burgoyne was at first incredulous, but on referring to Lady Burgoyne, who knew Dr. Evans well by name, he consented to receive the lady announced as the Empress, on condition of making his own arrangements and assuming all responsibility. Dr. Evans was extremely anxious that she should be taken on board immediately, fearing not only for the Empress, but also serious consequences for himself if he, as a foreigner, liable to expulsion at any time, were found in the act of aiding the Regent to leave the country. Sir John Burgoyne pointed out the immense danger of embarking the Empress in broad daylight, especially as the harbor of Deauville was tidal, and the yacht could not leave it till the top of high water. After some discussion, it was settled that the Empress should embark at midnight. At half-past eleven a police agent came on board and carefully examined every part of the yacht, at last leaving it perfectly satisfied that his suspicions were groundless. It is not known how he was first led to suppose that the Empress might be there. Sir John Burgoyne

[1] Deauville and Trouville are parts of the same town.

appeared perfectly indifferent, giving him every facility for examining the vessel, but naturally felt much relieved when he went on shore, and, after watching his proceedings through night-glasses, and seeing him cross the bridge leading to the Trouville side, he went on shore himself at the place appointed for meeting the Empress. Soon he saw two ladies walking together, followed by a gentleman (the nephew of Dr. Evans) carrying a hand-bag kindly prepared by Mrs. Evans, and containing traveling necessaries. One of the ladies immediately accosted him, saying, "I believe you are the English gentleman who will take me to England. I am the Empress," bursting into tears as she spoke. Sir John Burgoyne then told his name, and offering his arm led her on board the yacht *Gazelle*, where Lady Burgoyne was presented to her. She eagerly asked for news of the Emperor and Prince Imperial, and begged for newspapers. As she stepped on board, she seemed frightened, but on receiving the assurance that she was perfectly safe, she replied gracefully: "I am, I know, safe with an English gentleman." She spoke English, which she knew well, and often used in conversing with the Emperor, when she did not wish to be understood by those around her. Her pronunciation of that language was perhaps less foreign than her French, which she spoke with a marked Spanish accent.

She was much agitated on that evening, weeping frequently, as she spoke to Lady Burgoyne, saying that she had been shamefully deserted at the Tuileries, that her very servants had stolen things from her private apartments, and that on the fourth of September, the day of her flight, she could not even get her ordinary servants to bring her breakfast, and her ladies had to perform menial offices to help her. At the same time she showed fortitude, but perhaps more confidence than was quite justified by the circumstances, as six hours must elapse before the water would be high enough for the yacht to leave the dock. Sir John Burgoyne was exceedingly anxious, and in his fear of attracting attention by too much going to and fro, he desired Dr. Evans and his nephew to remain on board. There was great noise in the town, all regular government having ceased, and the place being full of drunken, disorderly *mobiles*, whose riotous appearance alarmed Sir John Burgoyne so much that he called up his men, told them who was the lady whom he had taken on board, and warned them that they might possibly be called upon to defend the Empress. The men all answered that they would do their duty.

Lady Burgoyne tried to persuade the Empress to take rest, but she was too much absorbed in her newspapers, and kept herself awake by drinking coffee. When the time came for leaving the harbor, the weather was so stormy that the crew became anxious as to the possibility of a small sailing-vessel like the *Gazelle* encountering such a sea without perishing in the attempt to cross the Channel. That very night the six-gun turret ship *Captain*, of the British navy, with five hundred men on board, commanded, through a curious coincidence, by Captain Hugh Burgoyne, cousin of Sir John Burgoyne, foundered off Cape Finisterre. The danger was great, but everything had to be risked under such circumstances, and at seven in the morning the yacht *Gazelle* set off on her adventurous passage, which lasted eighteen hours.

The nephew of Dr. Evans went on shore at six o'clock, but the latter, although he would have been fully justified in leaving the Empress under the care of Sir John Burgoyne, and although well aware of the danger, determined not to leave her till she had reached English soil, bravely risking his life in the attempt.

Sir John Burgoyne also imperiled the life of his wife, who nobly accepted her share of the immense danger, and had but one thought, the care of her illustrious charge, whom she encouraged by her example, showing no sign of fear, although the small yacht shipped heavy seas by which at any time it might have been swamped, and struggled against wind and weather. The Empress and Madame Lebreton both showed calm courage, but many times they thought they had seen their last of land. At the worst of the tempest, when, as Madame Lebreton said, "Tout craquait autour de nous" (Everything seemed to give way around us), the Empress remarked that the storm in Paris had been worse still.

Sir John Burgoyne remained on deck the whole time, commanding his yacht himself with able sea-

RUINS OF THE VESTIBULE OF THE TUILERIES.
FROM A PHOTOGRAPH.

manship, and at two o'clock in the morning of the eighth of September he safely brought the sturdy little vessel to Ryde, in the Isle of Wight, where they anchored. At three o'clock an excellent supper was served in the main cabin, where the Empress, now relieved from present anxiety, joined the party and was very cheerful. Her health was drunk in champagne, for which she returned thanks, expressing herself hopefully; but it was noticed that, now she had recovered her self-possession, she became extremely reticent in regard to political subjects, no longer complaining vehemently of those who had deserted her, or entering into the particulars of her grievances. She warmly expressed her gratitude to Sir John and Lady Burgoyne, and also her wish to give some token of her thanks to the crew. A gold piece of twenty francs (four dollars) to each man being considered sufficient by those around her, the men were summoned to the cabin, and each one received his gold piece from the hand of the Empress, who said as she gave it, in English, "I thank you very much." They were all delighted, but would not spend the coins, in which they punched holes to wear them as mementos.

At half-past seven the Empress landed with Sir John Burgoyne, after her soiled traveling-clothes had been replaced by more fitting attire supplied by Lady Burgoyne. She was taken at once to the York Hotel at Ryde, and from thence went over to Hastings, where she had the joy of meeting the Prince Imperial.

In a few days a group of Bonapartists formed a small court around her, and she settled at Camden Place, Chiselhurst, in a furnished country house placed at her disposal at a nominal rent by a wealthy Englishman named Strode. The Emperor was a prisoner at Wilhelmshöhe, but was kindly and courteously treated. He was, nevertheless, heartbroken, thinking only of the sufferings of the army, to whom he sent all the money he could raise. To the last the poor Emperor was generous and unselfish, thinking far more of the sufferings endured by others than of his own, cruel as they were. Even the Germans around him were completely won by his unvarying gentleness and patience, with the kindness ever ready to sympathize with all their own concerns, whether for weal or for woe.

CHAPTER XXIII

The Emperor in England — Visit of Lord Malmesbury — His impression of the interview — The Commune in Paris — What the leaders really were — Burning of the Tuileries — How effected.

THERE were great official difficulties in the way of the much-desired visit of the Empress to Wilhelmshöhe. At last, however, in December she determined to try a rapid journey, *incognita*, without informing any one of her intentions. This she managed to effect, but dared not take the Prince Imperial with her, notwithstanding his entreaties. Her arrival at Wilhelmshöhe was quite unexpected by the Emperor, who received her with a joy which he was obliged to conceal so as not to betray her identity. They were able, however, to converse together alone, and both derived great comfort from the short meeting. The capitulation of Paris and the treaty of peace, however, soon released the imperial prisoner, who then joined his wife and son at Chiselhurst.

We must again quote Lord Malmesbury, who, as an old friend, immediately went to see him:

"After a few minutes he came into the room alone, and with that remarkable smile which could light up his dark countenance, he shook me heartily by the hand. I confess that I never was more moved. His quiet and calm dignity, and absence of all nervousness and irritability, were the grandest examples of human moral courage that the severest stoic could have imagined.

"I felt overpowered by the position. All the past rushed to my memory: our youth together at Rome in 1829; his dreams of power at that time; his subsequent efforts to obtain it; his prison, where I found him still sanguine and unchanged; his wonderful escape from Ham; and his residence in London, where, in the riots of 1848, he acted the special constable like any Englishman; his election as president by millions in France in 1850; his further one by millions to the imperial crown; the glory of his reign of twenty years over France, which he had enriched beyond belief, and adorned beyond all other countries and capitals—all these memories crowded upon me as the man stood before me whose race had been so successful and romantic, now without a crown, without an army, without a country, or an inch of ground which he could call his own, except the house he hired in an English village.

"I must have shown, for I could not conceal, what I felt, as, again shaking my hand, he said: 'À la guerre, comme à la guerre.[1] C'est bien bon de venir me voir' (It is very kind of you to come to see me).

"In a quiet, natural way he praised the kindness

---

[1] A French proverb, meaning that we must bear the fortunes of war.

of the Germans at Wilhelmshöhe, nor did a single complaint escape him during our conversation. He said he had been *trompé* (deceived) as to the force and preparation of his army, but without mentioning names; nor did he abuse any one until I mentioned General Trochu, who deserted the Empress whom he had sworn to defend, and gave Paris up to the mob, when the Emperor remarked, 'Ah! voilà un drôle' (There is a villain). During half an hour he conversed with me as calmly as in the best days of his life. . . . When I saw him again in 1872 I found him much more depressed at the destruction of Paris, and at the anarchy prevailing over France, than he was at his own misfortunes; and that the Communists should have committed such horrors in the presence of their enemies, the Prussian armies, appeared to him the very acme of humiliation and national infamy."

His fate is now deeply regretted by the French of all classes, save a fraction of ardent republicans. If his son had lived he would, in all probability, govern France at the present time, for all love his memory, and all repeat how happy was the time of the Second Empire.

The horrors of the siege and of the Commune are not, perhaps, sufficiently known outside of France. They have been described by enthusiastic writers, taking a one-sided view of the terrible subject, and who have presented a totally false picture. That among the Communists were many sincere and well-meaning republicans, who, taking an imaginative view of events, indulged in fanciful, but cherished and honest dreams, is undeniable. It must also be admitted that in the frightful reprisals after the entry of the troops, there were many innocent victims— poor workmen, especially— who had acted perforce to give bread to their families. But the majority of the leaders were monsters, whose sole object was their own gain, and who savagely massacred what stood in their way, with deliberate, merciless cruelty.

Most of these men were governed by the mere hatred of what was above them, with the determination to enjoy everything which others had enjoyed, and to destroy, rather than lose, what they had gained by robbery, lest others should obtain the advantages which they now possessed. Under such circumstances it can be no matter of surprise that the last days of the Tuileries were at hand. Meanwhile, the sovereign people, proud of entering the palace of kings, went there for dreary fêtes during the siege and the Commune, while the "Marseillaise" was recited by the tragic actress Mlle. Agar, and a virago sang a street song, glorifying *la canaille*, "C'est la canaille! eh bien, j'en suis," a proposition that none felt inclined to deny.

But the palace of the Tuileries was soon to perish in a catastrophe recalling memories of Nineveh and Babylon.

Bergeret, the Communist leader, had declared that

the Tuileries would be in ashes before he left it, and he kept his word. No one else should enjoy what he could not have. On May 21, 1871, the Versailles troops entered Paris, and on the 23d Bergeret, in a war council, decreed the destruction of the palace. In this dreadful task he was assisted by a butcher named Bénot. During the afternoon of that fatal day omnibuses and carts loaded with gunpowder and petroleum repeatedly crossed the court of the Louvre and the Place du Carrousel, while their contents were thrown into the central pavilion of the Tuileries, called "Pavillon de l'Horloge." Bénot collected petroleum in pails, with candles and brushes, and led his associates through the splendid galleries, where they dashed petroleum over the hangings, the floors, walls, and doors. Here and there they placed jars of petroleum, a barrel of gunpowder on the ground floor, and a heap of combustible matter in the magnificent "Salle des Maréchaux." All was connected by trains of gunpowder.

When all was ready, with the delight of a madman Bénot set fire to the building. At a few minutes before nine the great clock stopped, under the influence of the fire. At ten o'clock the conflagration was raging in all its fury, while Bergeret and his so-called "officers" went quietly to dinner at the Louvre barracks, and then came out on the terrace to enjoy the sight of their fiendish work.

It was an awful, but magnificent spectacle. At eleven o'clock there was a terrific explosion, and the central cupola, the *chef-d'œuvre* of Philibert Delorme, fell in. At four o'clock in the morning the Communists, wishing to complete their work of destruction, set fire to the priceless library of the Louvre, despite the entreaties of the keepers, who shed tears as they saw treasures impossible to replace utterly destroyed. The whole building was threatened with destruction, including the picture-galleries and museums. Happily, MacMahon's troops arrived in time to save the latter.

But the palace of the Tuileries was a mere wreck, though beautiful still. The graceful outlines yet remained; the stones were not blackened, but reddened, by the flames, and seemed to bear a weird, lurid glow. The fire had done its work with strange caprice; here and there, amid the crumbling ruins, a wooden shutter or a piece of drapery had escaped. The hand of the clock dial still pointed to the fatal hour. Fragments of the velvet curtains embroidered with golden bees (the imperial emblem) could still be seen in the "Salle des Maréchaux," and also, in the apartments of the Empress, the crimson hangings of the canopy over her bed. Nothing but the mere front of the building remained, however, in any shapely form, and the internal destruction could easily be discerned from the exterior. Still this sad memento of civil war and savage passions was worthy of preservation; it was beautiful with the sad beauty of the ruins of Heidelberg. The halo of its glorious past seemed still to surround it; but

THE PAVILION OF FLORA AFTER THE FIRE.

This structure connected the Tuileries with the south, or Seine, wing of the Louvre.

greater than its beauty was the lesson it conveyed of the consequences of revolutionary anarchy.

The two pavilions at the extreme ends of the building have been restored: the Pavillon de Flore, looking on the quay and the Seine; the Pavillon Marsan, looking on the rue de Rivoli, where I lived for so many years! This has been entirely rebuilt; the Pavillon de Flore was less injured, and more easily repaired.

The whole of the central part of the building, the chapel, the splendid "Salle des Maréchaux," the apartments of the Emperor, Empress, and Prince Imperial, have been entirely pulled down, and the space on which they stood turned into a garden.

Flowers now bloom, and children play, on the spot where Marie Antoinette shed such bitter tears; where Madame Elisabeth tried to save her by the sacrifice of her own life; where Napoleon I. brought his glory and his imperial crown; where Josephine smiled and "won hearts" for her faithless hero; the palace from which the "King of Rome"[1] would not go when his mother, Marie Louise, fled before the allies, and from which he was torn by force, crying, "I will not leave my palace of the Tuileries!"[2] as if he foresaw he would never see it again; that palace whence two other monarchs fled in succession, swept away by a storm of revolution, and where, after many changes and reverses, the grand-

[1] Son of Napoleon I. and Marie Louise.
[2] The (Princesse) Comtesse de Tascher was present at this scene.

son of Josephine reigned, by the vote of the nation, with his beautiful consort, during a period of splendor, glory, and prosperity such as will never be seen again.

It is said that before leaving the Tuileries, the Empress Eugénie stood for a moment motionless, with fixed gaze, repeating as if unconsciously: "A dream! A dream! A hollow dream!"

CONCLUSION

The Empress and her son settle at Camden Place, Chiselhurst — The Emperor joins them after the peace — First difficulties — Education of the Prince Imperial — Woolwich — Hopes of a restoration of the Empire — The Emperor's health — His unexpected death — The Prince receives a large number of Imperialists on his coming of age — Passes his examination satisfactorily at Woolwich — His life at Chiselhurst — Difficulties — Hopes — He determines to join the English army in South Africa — His departure — His reckless bravery — He is killed in a reconnoissance — Particulars of his death — Announcement of the news to the Empress — Her journey to Zululand — Her present life.

THE residence of Camden Place, Chiselhurst, had been offered to the Empress Eugénie as a loan, by the owner, Mr. Strode, in her first hour of distressed perplexity on arriving in England as an exile. The Empress, however, insisted on paying rent; and after some discussion, Mr. Strode having finally accepted a nominal sum, the Empress and her son sorrowfully took possession of the shelter so quickly and providentially placed at their disposal. Here, the tutor of the Prince Imperial, M. Filon, immediately joined them, and the young Prince resumed his studies without delay. A few faithful followers, with members of the imperial family, gathered round them, while the Duchesse de Mouchy

(Princess Anna Murat) supplied the unfortunate Empress with the necessaries of which she was completely deprived, having nothing but what Mrs. Evans had put into a traveling-bag for her use, with the dress taken from Lady Burgoyne's wardrobe to replace the travel-stained garb in which she had fled from the Tuileries. The revolutionary government having, however, authorized the removal of her personal effects, they were speedily sent to her, and the strange inconveniences of her altered position ceased to exist.

The Emperor, being, as he said, determined to share the fate of the army, refused all offers of liberation till the signature of the treaty of Versailles, by which the French prisoners were released. When they were free, but not till then, the Emperor joined the Empress and his son in England, where he was received, even by the people, with great warmth and sympathy.

But the question of how they were to live was now the problem to be solved. The Emperor was proud to declare that all he had received from France had returned to France, and that he had taken nothing with him. After Sedan, and during his imprisonment at Wilhelmshöhe, all the money in his possession, or that he was able to raise by personal sacrifice, had been sent for the relief of the war-prisoners in Germany; he had nothing left. And this was fully characteristic of his nature from his earliest years. When a prisoner at Ham, during the reign of Louis Philippe, horse exercise had been ordered, medically, as necessary for his health; and although it could only be taken on the ramparts of the fortress, he greatly enjoyed this one resource of recreation. And yet he sold his horse to relieve the distress prevalent in the country around him.[1]

In the same spirit he gave all he had to relieve the sufferings of the captive army. If he had not, from time to time, purchased land for the purpose of agricultural experiments, and model farms, etc., he would have been penniless; but this private property, originally bought for philanthropic purposes, was now sold, and brought him the small fortune which we have before mentioned as having been sworn, on the Emperor's demise, in the Probate Court, as under £120,000.[2]

The straits from which he suffered at first were painfully depicted in a letter from Torquay, where he had been sent by his medical advisers in the hope that a milder climate might relieve the sufferings which had been greatly increased by the intense cold of Wilhelmshöhe. The Emperor stated that he had found benefit from the change,—that he would willingly remain longer; "but hotels are dear, and I must go back to Chiselhurst."

The Empress had considerable property in Spain, and went over to her native land in order to effect the sale of her estates. The Emperor wrote to her:

[1] See "Napoléon III. Intime," by Fernand Giraudeau.   [2] Ibid.

"It is, no doubt, very painful to part with what has belonged to your family for so long a time; but it is for the sake of our son's future."[1]

Immense sums of money had been at the disposal of the Emperor, who had never thought of his own interests. The horrors of the Commune, and the anarchy in France, affected him far more than his own misfortunes; but they raised hopes of a reaction in his favor, which he valued for his son's sake. These were encouraged by the reports of his few faithful followers — how few, alas! for the honor of human nature!

It is certainly true — and all those who were in France at that time can bear witness — that, notwithstanding the reverses of the Empire, what had followed was so horrible that regret for past peace and prosperity was really awakened; there was now a strong feeling of sympathy for the Emperor, and especially for the Prince Imperial — the "Petit Prince," whom all remembered with fond affection — the "Son of France."

Beyond a small minority, no one cared for the Comte de Chambord; and the large sum claimed by the Orléans princes as restitution, at the time when the coffers of the State were empty, and the nation was crushed by the terrible war-forfeit to Germany, had caused a general feeling of exasperation against them, which had greatly damaged their cause.

[1] Fernand Giraudeau.

The confiscation of the property of the Orléans family was certainly the least justifiable act of the Emperor's reign, and was so completely in contradiction to his generous nature and magnanimous spirit that it is impossible not to believe that it was suggested, and finally enforced, by unscrupulous advisers or too recklessly devoted partizans. But the time chosen by the Orléans princes for putting forward their just claims was most inopportune, and was universally resented.

Notwithstanding the symptoms of a Bonapartist reaction, the time had not yet come when a "return from Elba" could be risked; and the Emperor's greatest present care was the education of his son, superintended by himself, with the Prince's tutor, and the assistance of professors. The Emperor personally undertook to teach his son modern history compared with that of past times; and in long conversations he strove to develop his judgment, and to initiate him in political questions concerning the government of nations.

The Emperor no longer spoiled "Loulou," although, as ever, he was the kindest, the most affectionate of fathers — the friend and guide of his son, who, matured by adversity, now studied assiduously from seven o'clock in the morning till the same hour in the evening, with no other interruption than was necessary for the *déjeuner*, and two hours devoted to horse exercise. The whole imperial party lived at Chiselhurst in complete retirement, with only a few faithful attendants, who formed a small court around them, at the head of which was the Duc de Bassano, who had immediately followed the Empress after her flight, and a few servants, most of whom had come from the Tuileries.

The Emperor, however, soon felt that a more complete and more official course of instruction would be necessary for his son; and, notwithstanding the objection that an English military school would be unwelcome to his French supporters, having none other within his reach, he applied to the Queen of England for permission to send the Prince Imperial to the Royal Academy at Woolwich. The Queen not only heartily gave the necessary authorization, but offered to dispense with the preliminary examination. To this, however, the young Prince would not consent; and never did he accept any indulgence throughout the course of studies, although it is easy to understand that he labored under unusual disadvantages, having had only foreign methods and training, which differ from what is usual in England.

In October, 1871 — scarcely more than a year since his father's surrender at Sedan, and his mother's flight from the palace of his birth — after satisfactorily passing the usual examination, the Prince Imperial was admitted into the Royal Academy at Woolwich, with his young friend, Louis Conneau. Both had this explanatory note affixed to their names:

"Not as commissioned cadets, but as being authorized to follow the course of studies with the cadets."

The Prince would accept no favor of any kind, and in every respect was treated like his comrades.

In an interesting book by the Comte d'Hérisson, "Le Prince Impérial," he describes a visit to Woolwich after the death of the poor young Prince, and a conversation with General Simmons, who commanded the military school during his stay there. General Simmons spoke of him with the highest esteem and great affection. He explained to the Comte d'Hérisson the impossibility of showing any favor to a cadet in the examinations. The questions are prepared and sealed at the War Office. The cadets do not know beforehand the questions which will fall to them, and the examiners are equally ignorant of the authorship of the answers, which bear no signature, and are only marked by chance numbers.

The young Prince liked his new life at Woolwich, and according to universal testimony he won the good-will and esteem of all his English comrades.

Meanwhile, the chances of a Bonapartist restoration seemed to be ripening. An explanatory pamphlet on the war of 1870, published under the name of the Comte de la Chapelle, but really written by the Emperor himself, had been much discussed by the press, and had produced a general and strong impression. The former partizans of the Empire now raised their heads and drew around the Emperor, offering their services. The Comte de la Chapelle (who assisted the exiled sovereign in his desk-labors, and acted as his emissary in many political matters) succeeded in winning over other adherents; so that soon the Emperor felt that he was supported by a powerful political party, able to lead on the masses, where there might be hesitation, but no hostility. A plan of action was carefully prepared, and the success of an appeal to the nation seemed more than probable.

But the Emperor's health did not admit of the vigorous personal direction and coöperation which were necessary under such circumstances, and in the interest of his son, for whom he was ready to make any sacrifice, the Emperor consented to undergo the operation which was fated to have such a dire result. Although he had a nervous dread of the pain in prospect, he seems to have been kept in ignorance of the extent of the danger he had to encounter, and of which the Prince Imperial, especially, had no definite appreciation. He knew that his father had a serious internal malady, which prevented him from sharing his son's rides on horseback; the Prince knew also that surgical means had been considered necessary, but he was deceived by the perfect calmness of the Emperor, who showed no apprehension, and he did not foresee even the possibility of the calamity which was soon to befall him.

"*Dans un mois—à cheval!*" (A month hence—to horse!) said the Emperor, cheerfully, to the Comte de la Chapelle, only a few days before his death.

The operation, which was performed by the slow and gradual process, was endured by the Emperor, several times, with perfect success. A letter from the Emperor's French physician, Baron Corvisart, quoted by the Comte de la Chapelle, dated January 11, 1873, was full of satisfaction for the present, and hope for the future. He says:

"The Emperor has dined; he has no fever; all is going on as well as we could wish."

Sir Henry Thompson, the operating surgeon, had again successfully performed two operations, and the thirteenth of January was appointed for the final ordeal; but the condition of the Emperor seemed so favorable that the presence of the Prince Imperial was considered unnecessary, and on the twelfth he returned to Woolwich, little dreaming that he would never again see his father alive.

The prominent English physician who principally attended on this occasion (while Sir Henry Thompson's care was purely surgical) had ordered a draught, prepared with chloral, to be taken on the evening of the twelfth of January. The Emperor absolutely refused to take it, saying that the draught had thrown him into a distressing state of prostration on the previous night, that he felt no pain, and that, should it return, he would infinitely prefer to endure it rather than take the chloral.

But the order of the attending physician was stringent; the Empress was called, and her entreaties induced the Emperor to take the dose.

The chloral was taken at nine o'clock in the evening; the Emperor fell into a deep sleep, from which he only momentarily awakened at ten o'clock on the following morning; but he was then, evidently, fast sinking.[1] He uttered a few unintelligible words, and as the Empress anxiously bent over him he made a motion as if to kiss her, and immediately expired.

The grief and consternation of all around him were indescribable. The Comte de la Chapelle, from whose narrative we borrow these particulars, states that he arrived at Chiselhurst on that very morning, and was present at a sharp altercation between Sir Henry Thompson and the attending physician, on the subject of the dose of chloral. There was, unhappily, nothing to be done, and consequently the matter was hushed up.

The Comte Clary had immediately set off to bring the Prince Imperial, when the first alarming symptoms appeared, but of course all was over long before he could reach Chiselhurst. The Empress went to meet him, and her first sobbing words, as she embraced him: "My poor Louis, you are all I have left!" contained the first positive assurance that all was indeed over; that his beloved father, his best friend, had been taken from him.

The poor boy sobbed as if his heart would break

---

[1] The writer begs to leave the full responsibility of this narrative, and its conclusions, to the Comte de la Chapelle, not having the presumption to form a personal opinion.

as he embraced the lifeless form; but after a paroxysm of grief, by a truly Christian and affecting impulse, he fell on his knees, and repeated aloud the Lord's prayer.

At the solemn funeral of Napoleon III. the demeanor of the young heir of the Bonapartes awoke sympathy from all in the immense concourse of French, belonging to all classes, who came to offer a last mark of respect to their late sovereign. In an interesting paper on the Prince Imperial, published in the "Century Magazine" for June, 1893, Mr. Archibald Forbes thus describes the scene:

"I never saw dignity and self-control more finely manifested in union, than when the lad, not yet seventeen, dressed in a black cloak, over which was the broad red ribbon of the Legion of Honor, followed his father as chief mourner along the path lined by many thousand French sympathizers; and his demeanor was truly royal, when, later on that trying day, the masses of French artisans hailed him with shouts of 'Vive Napoléon IV.!'—and he stopped the personal ovation by saying: 'My friends, I thank you, but your Emperor is dead. Let us join in the cry of "Vive la France,"' baring at the same time his head, and leading off the acclamation."

The best proof of the Emperor's unconsciousness of his own danger may be found in the fact that no will was discovered of more recent date than one written in 1865, five years before the fall of the Empire, in which he left everything that he possessed as private property to the Empress, evidently supposing that his son would be his successor on the throne of France. It cannot be admitted that under such altered circumstances he would not have otherwise provided for his son, had he foreseen the possibility of a fatal issue to the operation.

The Empress was sole guardian of her son; for Prince Napoleon, who, according to the French law, as the nearest relative, should have represented the paternal line in watching over the interests of the young Prince, characteristically refused to have anything to do with him, and left England immediately after the funeral of the Emperor.

The young Prince then returned to Woolwich, where he studied assiduously, feeling that he was obeying the wishes of his father, for whose loss he could not be comforted.

A year later, having reached his legal majority of eighteen years, he received the deputations from the different provinces of France, each deputation headed by a leader, bearing the provincial banner. More than ten thousand Frenchmen of every class had gathered at Chiselhurst, led by sixty-five prefects of the Empire, many members of the National Assembly, and twelve former ministers. A tremendous shout of "Vive l'Empereur!" greeted the young heir as he appeared, with his mother by his side, surrounded by the leading Bonapartist statesmen, and the representatives of the highest classes of Imperialists during the Empire. After the address of the Duc de Padoue, expressing the faith of those around him in the future of the dynasty chosen by the nation, and bidding him to be prepared for what might, providentially, be in store for him, the young Prince, with a dignity and simplicity which greatly impressed all present, thanked them in the name of his father, recalling his principles and his teaching; he referred to the will of the nation, which should rise above all political parties, in the choice of what would best secure the public good; he alluded to his own youth with great modesty, and concluded with the following declaration: "When the hour has come, if another government should be preferred by the majority of the nation, I will bow respectfully to the decision of the country; but if the name of Napoleon, for the eighth time, should be chosen by the people, I am ready to accept the responsibility imposed upon me by the vote of the nation."

The enthusiasm aroused by this simple, manly speech spread far and wide.

The young Prince still required ten months of study to finish the course of instruction begun at Woolwich. Many of his advisers thought that, having taken the position of a Pretender, there would be some loss of dignity in returning even to a military school; but he was extremely anxious to pass his final examinations, and it was settled that he should resume his studies. How thoroughly he worked to carry out his father's views in sending him to Woolwich may be inferred from the fact that, in consequence of the before-mentioned disadvantages under which he labored, he had been twenty-second in a class of thirty-five during the year 1873; but when he left the Royal Academy in 1875, he had outstripped his competitors, and now held the position of seventh among thirty-five, with the option, had he entered the Queen's service, of choosing between the engineers and artillery.

On his return to Chiselhurst he became the official representative of the Bonapartist cause, but was, nevertheless, condemned to lead a life which could only be most irksome to a young man.

The Empress necessarily lived in retirement, and, like many other mothers, she did not sufficiently understand the craving for independence felt at the time of the approach to man's estate by all youths of any spirit. To the Empress he was still the child for whom strict discipline was necessary. Her position gave her complete control over him; and, with the idea of preserving him from the dangers of his age and rank, she fully exercised that control. She feared for him the example of the Prince of Wales and the young men of his court; she feared the treacherous allurements of French adventurers with wonderful plans for bringing about the restoration of the Empire; she feared the habits of the rich young English noblemen with whom he must associate; and, to guard against all these evils, she gave him as little money as possible. A small allowance for mere pocket-money was all that was granted to him, the Empress repeating in answer to all remonstrances: "Let him ask me for what he wants, and he shall have it." But what spirited lad of his age would submit to the necessity of always applying to his mother, and explaining his wishes — especially in a country where the "apron-string" is always mentioned with contempt? The Prince was a dutiful son, and did not rebel against his mother's will; but all agree in saying that he suffered acutely from the straits in which he was kept, and the humiliation of appearing as a pauper among the wealthy. A story is told by the Comte d'Hérisson of a dinner given by the Prince at St. James's Hotel, Piccadilly, to Count Schouvaloff, and to which he had invited General Fleury. The latter had brought with him Arthur Meyer, a young journalist, now editor of the "Gaulois" newspaper. This was unforeseen by the poor young Prince, whose supply of money had been reckoned so closely that when the bill had to be paid he was thirty shillings short, and was forced to borrow from General Fleury. The humiliation of such a necessity in the position of the young Prince will be understood by all. Another anecdote is related of a conversation with his former equerry, Bâchon, who, considering that the horse used by the Prince Imperial was not worthy of his rider, proposed to him another, costing six thousand francs ($1200). The Prince replied that he had not the money at his disposal; on which

Bâchon immediately offered to speak to the Empress, and lay the matter before her. The Prince quickly and decidedly forbade him to ask her for anything. An explanation followed; after which honest Bâchon, with tears in his eyes, declared that his Prince should have a suitable horse, and that he would pay for it himself by selling a small vineyard that he possessed. The Prince was much affected, but of course prevented the sacrifice of the vineyard.

In his will he left an annuity of five thousand francs ($1000) to his faithful Bâchon.

There is much to be said on both sides with regard to these delicate matters. The young Prince was deprived of his natural guide by the death of his father, and at the same time was raised to a particularly prominent and dangerous position at a too early age. His mother was certainly justified in fearing that he might be led into many errors. It is not easy under such circumstances to judge exactly how far it is wise to loosen the grasp of the reins. The Empress Eugénie held them with a firm hand. She feared the *naïveté*—what has been called "childishness"—of some points noticed in the character of the young Prince; and she did not understand that incessant dictation, incessant control, incessant watchfulness, would not tend to develop those qualities of determination in authority, and others necessary for a ruler of men. He was imaginative like his mother: "full of delusions," as Maxime

Du Camp (the well-known writer of the "Revue des Deux-Mondes") described him to me after a visit to Chiselhurst; although he admired his character in every respect, and repeated: "*Il est très bien.*"[1]

But the Prince was scarcely allowed to have an independent opinion, and was guided by others in all things.

He soon longed for emancipation. There was some question of a journey round the world, but various difficulties caused this plan to be given up. He traveled to Italy with his mother; to Sweden with the Comte Murat and his mother's devoted secretary, Franceschini Pietri. Wherever he went he gained the good will and esteem of all who were in contact with him. When he returned to the weary home at Chiselhurst he mixed in London society; but all this could not satisfy his yearning for decided action — his earnest wish to show himself the worthy representative of an illustrious name. Surely such feelings are high and noble, and should not be stigmatized as "ostentation," or else all the chivalry of past days must be open to the same accusation. He wished to show that he was not a mere carpet-knight, but a soldier in earnest, ready to "do his duty" fearlessly. But how, in his situation, could he get an opportunity of revealing the "sacred fire" that burned in his veins? He applied to the French government for permission to join

---

[1] In French the praise is higher than could be expressed by a literal translation, and signifies: "He is everything that he should be."

the troops fighting in Tonquin, but was refused; and meanwhile the sneers and ridicule heaped upon him by adverse French newspapers stung him to the quick. Nothing seemed open to him till the disaster of Isandlwana, and the hurried departure of English troops to retrieve the reverses in Zululand. Here, then, was the opportunity for which he had longed. His comrades of Woolwich were going — they would be exposed to the dangers of savage warfare; and he would not be a soldier of mere parade. He would share their peril, and would show his gratitude to the Queen of England by fighting under her flag. He did not stop to consider whether he would there be in the place belonging to a Bonaparte. He forgot the rancor of former times in present dreams of glory, and perhaps other "delusions" added to those already noted by Maxime Du Camp. The purpose, attributed by Mr. Forbes to the English court, of promoting the overthrow of the French Republic by giving the Prince an opportunity to distinguish himself is, according to my belief, a complete mistake. There is no more truth in the statement that there was a "project of marriage" between the Prince Imperial and a daughter of the Queen of England. There was, in fact, a youthful and delusive romance, but which no one contemplated seriously. The Queen, who had prevented the marriage of her niece[1] with Napoleon III., then at the zenith of prosperity, on the

[1] Princess Adelaide of Hohenlohe. See Memoirs of Lord Malmesbury.

ground of insecurity and difference of religious faith, would not be likely to unite her favorite daughter to the precarious fate of the exiled Prince Imperial.

That the Queen encouraged his wish to join the South African expedition is really true; but it may well be supposed that both the royal mother and the Prince of Wales — who did not foresee the too sad consequences of the consent given — were glad to welcome a natural interruption to a youthful love-story, which could not be taken into practical consideration. The sorrow, not unmixed with self-reproach, felt by the kind-hearted Queen, after the catastrophe, is well known. The ill-feeling, alluded to by Mr. Forbes, on the part of the French nation toward England since that time, is founded on the lamentable desertion of the young Prince, which caused his untimely fate, and not on any suspicion of a conspiracy or intrigue against the French Republic, every one being well aware that the part played by the English government in such matters has invariably been strictly neutral.

The young Prince told no one of his plans till they were definitely settled, and the earnest opposition of his friends and advisers could no longer prevail. The Empress herself knew nothing of his intentions till they were irrevocable. Several of the young Imperialists, who had been his personal friends, asked to follow him, and to form a sort of guard of honor around him. It is doubtful whether the English government would have consented to such an arrangement, but the proposal was never submitted to their examination, being, at once, characteristically rejected by the Empress, who replied: "My son goes as a soldier, and must share the fate of other soldiers, with equal protection, but no more."

On the eve of his departure from Chiselhurst, the young Prince summoned the domestic servants of the household around him, saying that before he left the country, for a long and perilous voyage, he wished to thank them for their services, and shake hands with them.

All shed tears, but they afterward remembered with renewed sadness how bright and hopeful he seemed, as he shook hands with each in turn, bidding them a hearty and friendly farewell.

The hurry of departure did not lead him to forget the duties incumbent upon all Catholics when about to encounter perilous adventures; and at an early hour in the morning he was seen running across the fields, to the Catholic chapel of Chiselhurst — the same where his remains were laid when brought back to England.

The rest of the sad tale is well known. His arrival in South Africa — especially intrusted to the care of Lord Chelmsford by the Commander-in-chief, the Duke of Cambridge; his appointment on the staff; his reckless bravery and love of enterprise, which led him several times into considerable danger, and which induced Lord Chelmsford to give

Colonel Harrison a *written order* that "the Prince should not quit the camp without a written permission *from his lordship*," says Mr. Forbes; who admits that "the military arrangements were lax," which is the sole possible explanation for the fact that, notwithstanding this prohibition, Colonel Harrison allowed him to go on the fatal reconnaissance with Lieutenant Carey. There seems to have been the grossest mismanagement throughout. No one appears to have clearly understood who was to command the expedition, Carey repudiating all responsibility, while Colonel Harrison maintained that he had intrusted the command of the escort to Carey. So far as it is possible to extract the truth from conflicting testimony, it would seem that Carey had the real command, but, as a matter of courtesy, left to the Prince the mere utterance of the orders, which came from himself. An escort of six white men and six Basutos had been requisitioned; but the latter never joined the party, thus reduced to the Prince, Lieutenant Carey, a sergeant, a corporal, four troopers, and a black native guide, nine persons in all.

The rest of the sad story may be briefly summed up, the facts being generally known: the imprudent sense of security of all the party, till the sudden surprise by the Zulus, before they had time to obey the order to mount; and the mad panic which caused a general flight, headed by Carey. It is best here to transcribe the graphic account given by Mr. Forbes:

"As to the Prince, the testimony is fairly unanimous. Sergeant Cochrane stated that he never actually mounted, but had foot in stirrup, when, at the Zulu volley, his horse, a spirited gray, sixteen hands high, and always difficult to mount, started off, presently broke away, and later was caught by the survivors. Then the Prince tried to escape on foot, and was last seen by Cochrane running into the donga [ravine], from which he never emerged. . . . The most detailed evidence was given by trooper Lecocq, a Channel islander. The Prince was unable to mount his impatient horse, scared as it was by the fire. One by one the troopers galloped by the Prince, who, as he ran alongside his now maddened horse, was endeavoring in vain to mount."

And not one of these men gave him a helping hand to hold the horse one moment, which would have enabled such a perfect horseman to vault into the saddle.

Mr. Forbes continues: "The Prince was left alone to his fate. The horse strained after that of Lecocq, who then saw the doomed Prince holding his stirrup-leather in one hand, grasping reins and pommel with the other, and trying to remount on the run. No doubt he made one desperate effort, trusting to the strength of his grasp on the band of leather crossing the pommel from holster to holster. That band tore under the strain. I inspected it next day, and found it no leather at all, but paper-faced — so that the Prince's fate was really attributable to shoddy saddlery. Lecocq saw the Prince fall backward, and his horse tread on him and then gallop

THE PRINCE IMPERIAL, IN ARTILLERY UNIFORM.
FROM A PHOTOGRAPH BY THE LONDON STEREOSCOPIC CO.

away. According to him, the Prince regained his feet, and ran at full speed toward the donga, on the track of the retreating party. When, for the last time, the Jerseyman turned round in the saddle, he saw the Prince still running, pursued only a few yards behind by some twelve or fourteen Zulus, assegais in hand, which they were throwing at him. None save the slayers saw the tragedy enacted in the donga."

When the Empress Eugénie went to see the spot where her gallant son had met his fate, the Zulus who had attacked him were discovered and questioned; they all said that when he saw he was forsaken and could not escape, "he turned on us like a young lion," and made a desperate defense. The body when found had seventeen wounds, one in the right eye, from an assegai, which the surgeons deemed was the first received, and immediately fatal. Let us hope that their appreciation is justified; but others stated that the wounds in the left arm seemed to have been received while holding it as a shield before his face. Mr. Forbes (an eye-witness of the scene) thus describes the finding of the body:

"He was lying on his back. His head was so bent to the right, that the cheek touched the sward. His hacked arms were lightly crossed over his lacerated chest, and his face, the features of which were nowise distorted, but wore a faint smile that slightly parted the lips, was marred by the destruction of the right eye from an assegai stab."

He adds: "His wounds bled afresh as we moved him. Round the poor Prince's neck his slayers had left a little gold chain, on which were strung a locket set with a miniature of his mother, and a reliquary containing a fragment of the true cross which was given by Pope Leo III. to Charlemagne when he crowned that great prince emperor of the West, and which dynasty after dynasty of French monarchs had since worn as a talisman."

The body was taken back to the camp, wrapped in a cloak and placed on the lance-shafts of the cavalrymen; and after embalmment, such as could be practised under the circumstances, and a solemn funeral service in the camp, the homeward journey began, which was to be principally effected on board of the *Orontes*, whence the bier was transferred at Spithead to the Admiralty-yacht *Enchantress*, which carried it to Woolwich, where funeral honors began.

Immediately after the catastrophe the Queen was informed by telegram sent to Balmoral, and she at once set off on her return journey to Windsor. By order of the Queen, Lord Sidney went to Chiselhurst to inform the French suite of the terrible news, and to urge them to prepare the Empress for a calamity which might be too suddenly revealed by some accidental circumstance. But no one could summon courage to inflict such a blow. The Duc de Bassano,[1] overpowered by his own personal grief—

---

[1] The following particulars were related to the writer by the Duc de Bassano himself.

for he was deeply attached to the poor young Prince
—implored Madame Lebreton to break the news to
the bereaved mother. "You are a woman: you will
know better what to say to her—how to prepare
and to comfort her." But Madame Lebreton vehemently retorted, "I should drop down dead in her
presence before I could utter the words!"

Meanwhile, the Empress seems to have heard
vaguely that a telegram had been received addressed
to her secretary, Pietri, who was absent; and during
the before-mentioned discussion she sent for the Duc
de Bassano, who had no choice left but to obey the
summons.

"Bassano," said the Empress, "what is this about
a telegram received? Have you news from Zululand?"

"Yes, Madame," answered the Duke mournfully,
"and the news received—is not good."

"What? Is my son ill?" asked the Empress
eagerly.

"There has been an engagement," faltered the
Duke.

"Is Louis wounded?"

"Yes."

"We must go to him directly," cried the Empress,
starting up. "Preparations must be made immediately; we must go up to London and embark for
the Cape. Give orders at once, my dear Duke!"

"But, Madame, how are we to embark? Ships
do not leave every day for the Cape."

"Oh, we shall find means — we can hire one if necessary."

"But such arrangements would require time — and — your Majesty *would arrive too late.*"

The Empress turned and looked full in the Duke's face, down which tears were flowing. She uttered a cry, and fell as if stricken by a thunderbolt; he was just in time to receive her in his arms.

I shall never forget the tone of anguish in which the Duc de Bassano said, when relating the above:

"I had rather be shot any day than go through such a scene again."

The crushing grief of the unfortunate mother was continually revived during the torturing weeks preceding the arrival of her son's remains by receiving his letters, sent by the mails before the telegram announcing the catastrophe. She could not open them till some time had elapsed. The last, written in pencil, was dated on June 1st, immediately before starting on the fatal reconnaissance.

The contrast between the bright and joyous tone of these letters and the circumstances in which they were received was heartbreaking to the mother when, at last, she opened these messages from the dead.

The magnificence of the funeral need not be described. It was a poor atonement; but such as it was, the English nation could offer no more, and their sympathy was heartily given. The Queen and Princess Beatrice wept "so bitterly that they could hardly stand," was the expression used by the Duc de Bassano. All France had sent deputations with funeral wreaths, and Englishmen of all ranks attended in crowds. The only person present who preserved his composure was Prince Napoleon, who refused to see the Empress after the ceremony, and immediately left England for Paris.

It is known that the Empress has now left Chiselhurst, where all the recollections awakened were too painful, and is settled at Farnborough, not far from Windsor, where she finds comfort in the sympathy and friendship of the Queen. The remains of her husband and son have been transferred to Farnborough. She lives in retirement with Madame Lebreton, her secretary, Pietri, and one or two other faithful followers. The Duc de Bassano, having reached a very advanced age, is now replaced in his official capacity by his son, the Marquis de Bassano, who accompanied the Empress in her sad pilgrimage to the spot where her son fell so gallantly, and where she seemed to find a sort of consolation in gathering every detail, every testimony, which could still further honor his memory.

No one seems to be exactly acquainted with her present financial position; but judging from appearances it may be supposed to be one of liberal comfort. The sale of her private jewels produced a large sum, and her own fortune is considerable. Her residence at Farnborough is handsome and well arranged; she has, also, a villa near Mentone, which is described as a paradise, where she seeks a refuge from English winters. But the life of the Empress Eugénie is ended. After having known the most exceptional prosperity ever granted to any woman, she remains alone and almost forgotten, save by a few faithful friends — having lost all that she prized as an Empress, all that she loved as a woman. What is left to her can scarcely be valued or enjoyed after such reverses.

Some of those who wish her well regret that she should have chosen to live on French ground in her southern home; and still more that she should now reappear in Paris, where once she reigned supreme, in a hired dwelling opposite to the vacant spot where the Tuileries once stood. This regret is increased by the fact that she is not popular in France, and that the part she played during the Empire is judged with unjust malevolence.

Eugénie de Montijo was raised to an unnatural elevation, for which nothing in her past life or education had prepared her; and if all circumstances be considered, it must be allowed by all who are not blinded by prejudice that few women could have gone through such an ordeal without having more cause for self-reproach. A woman so beautiful, so flattered, so admired, and so deeply wounded by her husband's errors, who yet never fell from her high estate, notwithstanding every temptation; one so spoiled by fortune as to be able to indulge in every caprice, and who was ever kind and charitable; who, after being betrayed and deserted by those whom she trusted, has no unkind word for the traitors, nor has ever sought for revenge; whose errors were those of a high and noble nature, ill regulated by defective guidance, but not the less real — such a woman deserves respect in the present and indulgence for the past.

She was dazzled by the splendor of her exalted position; for a time she thought only of pleasure and enjoyment, but no bad act can be laid at the door of the Empress Eugénie. Her faults were trifles in themselves, and became important only in consequence of the obligations of a situation which she never completely understood.

She has now suffered the deepest sorrow; she has lost all for which she was so much envied. Let us hope that her last years may be spent in peace.

www.ingramcontent.com/pod-product-compliance
Lightning Source LLC
Chambersburg PA
CBHW031852220426
43663CB00006B/588